D0836333

Stadium Stories:

Green Bay Packers

Stadium Stories™ Series

Stadium Stories:

Green Bay Packers

Colorful Tales of the Green and Gold

Gary D'Amato

GUILFORD, CONNECTICUT

Stadium Stories is a trademark of Morris Book Publishing, LLC.

Text design: Casey Shain
Cover photo of LeRoy Butler courtesy Sports Marketing & Management Group; all others by Vernon Biever

Library of Congress Cataloging-in-Publication Data
D'Amato, Gary, 1956–
    Stadium stories : Green Bay Packers : colorful tales of the green and gold / Gary D'Amato.–1st ed.
        p. cm. – (Stadium stories series)
    ISBN 0–7627–2745–4
1. Green Bay Packers (Football team)–History. I. Title: Green Bay Packers. II. Title. III. Series.
    GV956.G7D357 2004
    796.332'64'0977561–dc22

                                        2004040518

Manufactured in the United States of America
First Edition/First Printing

For my father, the biggest Packer fan of them all.

Contents

The World's Best Fans 1

Lombardi's Foot Soldiers 14

Lambeau Field Forever 32

For Biever, It's All Black and White 48

Lombardi Avenue, Memory Lane 62

The Quintessential Packer 74

Chester Marcol: Alive and Kicking 93

Tony Mandarich's Comeback 110

LeRoy Butler: Safety First 122

The One and Only 135

The World's Best Fans

Although he probably would not describe it in such terms, Mark Wagner has one of the easiest jobs in the National Football League. In fact he has one of the easiest jobs in all of professional sports.

Wagner is the director of ticket operations for the Green Bay Packers. His job, basically, is to sell tickets. This is not to suggest his job is stress-free, but Wagner faces few of the occupational hazards so common in his line of work.

He does not have to worry about a decline in attendance due to the Packers' performance or won–lost record. He does not have to worry about sagging ticket sales in a sluggish economy. He does not have to worry about planning and executing slick marketing campaigns to help sell tickets. He does not have to worry about discounting tickets to drive sales and determining what that would mean to the bottom line.

Wagner has none of those worries because the Packers have sold out every home game at Lambeau Field since 1960. Furthermore, there are nearly 60,000 names on the waiting list for season tickets and, in a typical year, approximately fifteen people decide, for whatever reason, not to renew their tickets. At that rate of turnover, Wagner can work about 4,000 more years, give or take a decade, before the current waiting list is exhausted.

Wagner does, however, have one job-related concern. "Sometimes, it's hard because you cannot satisfy the needs," he said. "But, yes, it's a nice problem to have."

The Oakland Raiders have the Raider Nation. The Dallas Cowboys, New York Yankees, and Chicago Cubs have large national and even international fan bases. Notre Dame's storied football program has millions of fans and its own national television contract. In fact most universities and professional sports franchises boast legions of loyal followers.

But there is nothing in American sport that quite compares with the bond that exists between the Packers and their fans.

Perhaps that bond exists because the team is located in what is by far the smallest market in the National Football League. Perhaps it exists because the Green Bay Packers are the only major sports franchise that is community owned. Perhaps it exists because the team is an important source of city, state, and regional pride. Perhaps it exists because the Packers date to 1919, and four generations have grown up following the team. Great-Grandpa cheered for Curly Lambeau and Buckets Goldenberg; Grandpa cheered for Don

Fingertip Catches

The Packers' Web site, www.packers.com, consistently ranks among the National Football League's five most frequently visited sites. Launched in 1997, packers.com also has been ranked among the top ten sites of the 121 official major professional team Web sites in the NFL, National Basketball Association, National Hockey League, and Major League Baseball.

Hutson and Tony Canadeo; Dad cheered for Bart Starr and Ray Nitschke; and little Johnny and Jenny cheer for Brett Favre and Kabeer Gbaja-Biamila.

More than likely, it is a combination of those factors—geography, tradition, culture—that explains the species *Packerus backerus* or "cheeseheads," as the team's supporters have come to be known in more recent years.

It's become somewhat fashionable for Packers fans to reinforce the image by sporting hats made of yellow foam—cheesy, in more ways than one—but the passion that inspires such displays of loyalty is anything but a passing fad. "Unlike most of the NFL teams, the Packers have generational fans," said John Carpentier, who is in the business of selling, buying, and trading Packers memorabilia and has written a book on the subject. "We have grandparents and parents that have passed down the passion to their kids and their grandkids."

The fact that the Packers are the only game in town helps fuel the fire. The closest major college football program is a two-and-one-half-hour drive away, at the University of Wisconsin. The closest National Basketball Association and Major League Baseball teams are located in Milwaukee, some 120 miles to the south.

"Green Bay is the smallest market in professional sports," Carpentier said. "Most of the other NFL cities have a lot of other sports and venues. They've got professional baseball teams and hockey teams and basketball teams. In Green Bay it's football, or football, or Packers football. And that's it. So the passion here runs much higher than anywhere else, and the loyalty to the players and the team runs higher."

Thanks to the globalization of the National Football League, however, cheeseheads are not confined to the Fox River Valley in Wisconsin. They live virtually all over the world. Carpentier said Packers fans from eighteen countries have visited his store, Stadium Sports & Antiques, located just two blocks from Lambeau Field. Packers season ticket holders live in all fifty states. Four have addresses in Alaska, three live in Hawaii, and five live in Canada. One man on the waiting list lives in Japan, according to Wagner.

"I have friends from Iowa who come in every year for a game," said Packers president Bob Harlan. "This is the biggest weekend of the year for them. This is Christmas for them. There's an attraction here that really appeals to people. It's the closest thing in the NFL to a college atmosphere, and I think that adds a warmth to it.

"It's just a good story. I always tell people [the Packers' story] is more fiction than reality, and in many ways, it is."

On game days, even in December, when snow is blowing horizontally and the windchill factor is below zero, the parking lot surrounding Lambeau Field is filled hours before kickoff. Fans warm their hands over charcoal grills, eat bratwurst, drink beer, and talk Packers football. Other teams may have groups of dedicated tailgaters, but in terms of numbers and style, nobody does pregame like Packers fans.

During the 2002 season a sportswriter from Holland, who was visiting several NFL cities for a series of stories he was writing about sports in America, was taken aback by the enthusiasm for the tailgating ritual in Green Bay. As is true of many aspects of the Packers experience, tailgating has to be seen to be believed.

After the fans are sated with high-cholesterol foods and copious amounts of alcohol, they file into Lambeau Field, which quickly swells to capacity. The fans, clad in snowmobile suits and blaze-orange hunting vests, sit on simple bench-type aluminum seats with no backs, sip from smuggled flasks, and cheer their frozen lungs out.

Packer fans take their tailgating seriously, as evidenced by this sign. It's a safe bet that the privately owned parking lot — and the advertised facilities—get plenty of use on game days. (Courtesy Gary D'Amato)

And the Packers also are one of the NFL's top draws on the road.

In Phoenix, where a large number of Midwesterners have relocated, it is not unusual to see thousands of spectators dressed in green and gold in the stands at Sun Devil Stadium when the Packers are in town to play the Arizona Cardinals.

Before the Tampa Bay Buccaneers started winning regularly in the 1990s, Packers fans sometimes outnumbered and outcheered Bucs fans in their own stadium, a source of great embarrassment to Tampa Bay's owners and players.

Fans from Michigan display their allegiance to the Packers during the 1966 NFL title game against the Dallas Cowboys. The team's fan base is spread from coast to coast—and beyond. (Vernon J. Biever Photo)

Many Packers fans take to the road to watch the team because tickets are easier to obtain in Detroit or Chicago than they are in Green Bay. A $295 million renovation of Lambeau Field, completed in time for the start of the 2003 season, will only put a dent in the season ticket waiting list.

Packers season tickets can be passed down from one generation to the next or transferred to immediate family members, but they cannot be transferred or willed to a non-family member.

Tickets have been the source of family disputes and have been contested in divorces.

Not surprisingly, given the intensity of the fans' loyalty and their desire to be identified with the team they support, the Packers are among the top teams in the NFL in sales of officially licensed merchandise and apparel. In the fiscal year that ended in March 2002, the Packers sold $6.1 million in merchandise.

Stop in any bar or shopping mall within a 100-mile radius of Green Bay during the regular season, and it's a safe bet that 50 percent of the people you encounter will be wearing at least one item of Packers clothing.

Carpentier said that when he obtains and puts up for sale items from the famous "Ice Bowl" game, which pitted the Packers against the Dallas Cowboys for the 1967 NFL title, fans are awestruck. "People touch them almost with a reverence," he said. "They joke sometimes, when we have an Ice Bowl ticket or program or souvenir from the game, that they can still feel the frost on it."

To truly understand the unique bond between the Packers and their fans, one has to go back to the beginning. When the team was founded in 1919, Green Bay was a hard-working paper mill town with a population of 31,017. Early on, there was a David versus Goliath aspect to almost every game. Although the franchise struggled to remain solvent, every time it appeared the Packers would go under, the community rallied enough support to keep it going.

On November 4, 1922, Andrew B. Turnbull, general manager of the *Green Bay Press-Gazette*, advanced Lambeau, the Packers' cofounder and coach, funds to cover guarantees in the event that rain canceled the game the next day against Columbus. After that season Turnbull recruited local businessmen and turned the Packers into a nonprofit corporation. The first stock sale, in August of 1923, raised $5,000.

A few years later, a lawsuit by a fan who suffered injuries resulting from a fall from the bleachers nearly put the team out of business. The court awarded the fan $5,000, but the Packers' liability insurance company had been a victim of the Great Depression. The team needed an additional $2,500 to settle with creditors.

Circuit Court Judge Henry Graass turned the franchise into receivership under Frank Jones, a Packers stockholder who allowed the team to be reorganized, going from the Green Bay Football Corporation to Green Bay Packers, Inc. In 1935 Lee Joannes, the team president, organized another stock drive that netted $15,000, allowing the Packers to pay off all team debts.

That the team managed to survive those early years, with fans literally passing the hat at games to raise funds to keep the franchise going one more week and one more year, is a big part of the Packers' mystique. The fans felt, and still feel, that they were and are an integral part of the team's successes and setbacks. The emotional attachments that stem from this form of "ownership" cannot be overstated.

"A player who is on our bench all the time can go some-place else as a free agent, and I'll get phone calls and letters: 'What's happening? What's going wrong?' " said Harlan, who answers his own phone and frequently takes calls from concerned fans. "I'll call them back and say, 'You know, it's not the end of the world. Brett [Favre] isn't leaving. Don't get so upset about it.'

"It's amazing. I will get four- and five-page handwritten letters from fans. How can they possibly have that many questions about one football team? But they do. What are we going to do about this? What are we going to do about that? They're very,

Help Wanted

Ever wonder who removes snow from the Lambeau Field bleachers when the inevitable December blizzard blows through? The citizens of Green Bay, that's who.

After a significant snowfall the Packers usually take out an advertisement in local newspapers, asking the fans to help. In recent years the team has paid fans $7.00 an hour for snow removal. The fans must bring their own shovels, and the job is so popular the team often has to turn away dozens of people.

very concerned. But I guess you'd be more upset if they weren't concerned and if they weren't interested in writing to you."

In 1997, during the height of the Packers' resurgence under General Manager Ron Wolf and Coach Mike Holmgren, the team's stockholders approved a plan for the issuance of additional stock for the first time since 1950. Each share cost $200. The five-month sale, which ended March 16, 1998, yielded nearly 106,000 new shareholders and added $24 million to the team's coffers.

As of 2003 a total of 4,748,909 shares were owned by 110,901 stockholders, none of whom receives any dividend on the initial investment. The stockholders didn't invest in the team to make money. They invested on an emotional level, to be able to say that they own a piece of the team they love. When the Packers sign a free agent, each stockholder can thump his chest and say, "I helped bring that guy to Green Bay."

"I own one share of stock," Harlan said. "I'm just like probably 80 percent of the people in the stadium on Sunday afternoon. We're all the same. We love the franchise, and we want to see it succeed."

The Packers' annual meeting is held at Lambeau Field, the only building in Green Bay large enough to accommodate the turnout of stockholders. The meeting has the look and feel of an oversized pep rally.

The fans who own shares of stock or season tickets are fortunate to have direct connections to the team, but affection for the Green Bay Packers literally spans the globe. A reporter who covers the team for the *Milwaukee Journal Sentinel* corresponds regularly with a Packers fan who teaches English in Shanghai, China. The man is an American citizen but has had numerous addresses in Europe and Asia. How did he become a Packers fan? He lived on the East Coast as a child during the 1960s and became fascinated with the teams coached by Vince Lombardi.

James Breeden is another Packers fan whose story is both atypical and familiar. Breeden lives in Mount Washington, Kentucky, and is a Kentuckian through and through. Though he lives in closer proximity to the Cincinnati Bengals, Tennessee Titans, St. Louis Rams, and Indianapolis Colts, Breeden bleeds green and gold. "I've been a Packers fan ever since I was born, practically," he said. "When I was a kid, they would show those games between the Packers and the Lions on Thanksgiving Day. That would have been in the early '50s, when TV was in its infancy. The Packers weren't even a good team, but I just picked up on them being this little team from nowhere, and I started to follow them. They became my favorite team."

That may be a bit of an understatement. When Breeden and his wife made a pilgrimage to Green Bay in the 1980s, they immediately fell in love with the city and the area. Their visits became more regular, and they started attending games, usually with tickets they got from sympathetic season ticket holders or even Packers players.

"Believe it or not, Tony Canadeo got my first two tickets for me," Breeden said, referring to the late Packers Hall of Fame running back. "We found out where he lived in Green Bay and just dropped in on him. He and his wife, Ruth, accepted us for who we were, and it just started a friendship."

The Breedens' visits to Titletown became so frequent they eventually bought a house on Wilson Street, barely a mile from Lambeau Field, so they wouldn't have to stay in hotels. The house is unoccupied except during the weeks the Breedens are in town.

"I've got good neighbors," Breeden said. "I keep the heat on, and my neighbors keep an eye on the place. It's home away from home. I've been in the tire business for about forty years in Mount Washington. When I'm gone, everybody knows where I'm at."

In 2002, Breeden finally got Packers season tickets. No, he didn't circumvent the waiting list; Breeden estimates there are still some 18,000 names ahead of his. "A friend of mine in Austin, Texas, his name had come up on the list but he's got an illness that keeps him close to home," Breeden said. "We've been friends for fifteen years. So he called and said, 'Jim, I'm in line for season tickets. Of course they have to stay in my name, but would you be interested in going in on the tickets?' So he gets the tickets in his name, we give him the money, and we get the tickets. It's quite an arrangement. It's a friendship arrangement."

It is an arrangement built on a mutual love for a team that plays its games half a country away from both the ticket owner and the ticket user.

Package Deals

The Packers have maintained two separate season ticket packages since 1995, when the four games played annually at Milwaukee County Stadium were moved to Lambeau Field: "Gold" ticket holders, primarily former Milwaukee patrons, have a three-game package consisting of the annual Midwest Shrine preseason game, plus the second and fifth regular-season home games each year. "Green" ticket holders, primarily original Green Bay patrons, have a seven-game package consisting of the annual Bishop's Charities preseason game and the remaining six regular-season games.

"I talk to people around the country who fly in for games," Harlan said. "I talk to a gentleman on the East Coast from time to time; he flies in for every game. I know people who drive in for games [from out of state]. That's not easy to do, particularly in December. They just don't want to give up their tickets. They know if they do, they will never get them back.

"We've sold out every game since 1960. We've still got over 50,000 names on our waiting list. We're going to increase our seating capacity to 71,000 [in 2003], and we're still going to have over 50,000 names on the waiting list for tickets. We've got waiting lists for club seats, for private boxes, and for seats in the bowl."

There isn't a professional sports franchise in America that wouldn't love to have the Packers' problems. Many other teams sell out home games for an entire season, for five seasons, even for ten seasons consecutively. But what other team can claim to have sold out every home game for more than four decades?

"Packers fans love the team, win or lose," Carpentier said. "That's something that I think is stronger here in Green Bay than anywhere else in the country, in any other NFL franchise. People know that these aren't finicky fans. Once you're a Packers fan, you're a Packers fan for life. With other teams people jump on and off the bandwagon. It seems that the Packers have something those other teams don't have: loyalty.

"No matter whether the team is winning or losing, the fans have that same passion. They never give up hope that the Packers are going to win another Super Bowl, another championship."

Speaking of championships, the Green Bay Packers have won twelve of them, more than any other NFL franchise. "When we won the Super Bowl in 1997, [NFL Commissioner] Paul Tagliabue came to town that spring, and he talked to our executive committee in our boardroom," Harlan said. "And he said, 'You know, Green Bay winning the Super Bowl is the best thing that's happened to pro sports in a long time. Because it's small-town America. It's blue-collar America. The team is owned by the fans.' He said, 'It took everybody back to a simpler time.'

"And I think that's exactly what this franchise does for people. It is little, and it's owned by the fans. It's the little guy against the big guy. People love this story, because of what the story is."

Lombardi's Foot Soldiers

B art Starr. Ray Nitschke. Willie Davis. Paul Hornung. Jim Taylor. Willie Wood. Herb Adderley. Forrest Gregg.

They are names that conjure up grainy images of the 1960s Green Bay Packers, who dominated the National Football League and served as a touchstone for a nation adrift in a sea of social unrest and fighting an increasingly unpopular war in Vietnam.

They are names that even today bring smiles to the faces of Packers fans, most of whom are well versed in the team's extraordinary success under Coach Vince Lombardi.

They are names associated with the Pro Football Hall of Fame in Canton, Ohio.

They are giants of the game, heroes, champions, icons.

For every Starr and Nitschke, however, there were dozens of players who passed through Green Bay from 1959 to 1967 and contributed in their own way to the legend of "Titletown, U.S.A."

Lombardi surely had his share of superstars, or the Packers would not have won five NFL titles during his nine seasons as head coach. But every field general also must have good foot soldiers, the anonymous grunts who toil in the trenches, carry out their assignments without question, and ultimately determine whether battles—and games—are won or lost.

For Lombardi they were players such as Bob Long, Jim Temp, and Gary Knafelc.

Unless you are an especially knowledgeable Packers fan, those names probably do not resonate. Starr and Nitschke will live forever in highlight reels and in the retelling of stories from one generation to the next. Long, Temp, and Knafelc are long forgotten by most, their career achievements mere footnotes in one of the greatest dynasties in sports.

"They started this legends group, which supposedly is all the guys who played for Lombardi, but it's really all the Hall of Famers, plus Jerry Kramer and Bob Skoronski and a couple other guys," said Temp, who played defensive end for the Packers from 1957 to 1960. "Sometimes they have public functions, autograph signings and such, and they ask us to come. You feel like such a jerk, because who the hell knows Jim Temp? It's embarrassing."

"Everyone wants to hear about Starr and Nitschke," said Long, a reserve flanker for the Packers from 1964 to 1967. "But there are a lot of guys like me who have good stories that we never get to tell. Nobody ever asks me about those stories."

Temp and Knafelc were in Green Bay when Lombardi was hired and played roles in the Packers' return to prominence in the league. Long played only four years in Green Bay but was a member of three NFL championship teams, including the winners of Super Bowls I and II.

Knafelc will never forget his introduction to Lombardi, at a hockey game in Green Bay shortly after the Packers hired the coach in 1959. "Lombardi was there with his wife, Marie, and Verne Lewellen [the team's general manager from 1954 to 1958]," Knafelc said. "Verne introduced me to Lombardi and I said kind of flippantly, 'I hope I can play half as well for you as Frank did.'"

Lombardi had been an assistant coach for the New York Giants and had coached Frank Gifford.

"Lombardi just kind of scowled at me," Knafelc said. "Then he said, 'How much do you weigh?' I lied and said, 'Oh, about 225.' He said, 'Meet me in my office tomorrow. You're going to be my tight end.' I said, 'Coach, I've been a flanker all these years.' He said, 'Well, now you're my tight end.' "

Knafelc reported to Lombardi's office as instructed and futilely protested his move to tight end. As the team's flanker he had caught the final touchdown pass in old City Stadium in 1956 and the first touchdown pass in new City Stadium (later renamed Lambeau Field) in 1957. Knafelc might as well have been talking to the door. As far as Lombardi was concerned, Knafelc was a tight end, and that was that.

"The very next day, Bill Howton called me," Knafelc said. "He said, 'Vince called me and wants to have lunch.' I said, 'First of all, Bill, I sure as hell wouldn't call him 'Vince.' I met him last night, and this guy doesn't mess around.' "

Howton, a wide receiver, had played for the Packers since 1952 and was the team's best offensive weapon. In his seven years in the league, he had caught 303 passes for 5,581 yards [an 18.4 average] and 43 touchdowns.

But in those seven years, the team had compiled a 26–56–2 record, and in 1958, the year before Lombardi arrived, the Packers were a woeful 1–10–1 under Coach Ray "Scooter" McLean. Howton and some other veterans ran roughshod over McLean, who was too nice to put them in their place.

Lombardi undoubtedly knew all about Howton's skills, on and off the field.

"I picked up Bill at the airport, and I had to run a few errands," Knafelc said. "When I got home, my wife said, 'Bill called and he wants you to pick him up.' I said, 'I just dropped him off.' She said, 'Well, he wants you to pick him up.' So I drove to the Packers offices downtown, and Bill was standing on the curb. I said, 'How did it go?' He just said, 'It went OK.'

"The next day, I found out Lombardi traded him to Cleveland. We were shocked. Bill was by far our best player, our best offensive threat. I remember Paul Hornung saying, 'Man, if he got rid of Howton, nobody is safe.' "

Said Temp: "Lombardi got rid of Billy Howton right off the bat because Howton was the clubhouse lawyer. Poor Scooter McLean. Howton would tell Scooter that he was working us too hard and our legs were gone. Well, my legs were gone with Lombardi, but they always came back."

If Lombardi had not made the point that he was in charge in Green Bay, there would be no doubt at the first team meeting, on the eve of training camp in 1959. "He said, 'There are trains, planes, and buses leaving Green Bay every day, and you may be on one of them,' " Temp said. "That morning at St. Norbert College, everything changed. I'll never forget it."

Knafelc was in the room that day and was left with the same lasting impression.

"He gave us that talk: 'I've never been associated with a loser, and I won't be associated with a loser in Green Bay,' " Knafelc said. "I never saw a whole group of men looking at each other with wide eyes like I did that day. But I don't think any of us had a negative thought. It wasn't like, 'Who is this crazy guy?' It was a feeling of expectation."

The Packers finished with a 7–5 record in 1959, their first winning season in twelve years. Two years later, they won the first of five NFL championships under Lombardi.

True to his word, Lombardi switched Knafelc to tight end, a position the coach helped revolutionize. Before Lombardi schemed to move one of his ends in close to the tackle to help

Gary Knafelc (84) shows off his pass-receiving skills during a photo session at training camp in the early 1960s. Knafelc caught the last touchdown pass at old City Stadium in 1956 and the first touchdown pass at what is now Lambeau Field in 1957. (Vernon J. Biever Photo)

block in the power running game, most teams lined up with two split ends and a flanker.

"Lombardi had a strong-side end, a blocking end, and that's where the term 'tight end' came from," Knafelc said. "The Bears used to have a slot back, but there was really no designated tight end until Lombardi."

The Packers sweep, the play that became Green Bay's bread and butter, was based in large part on the block of the tight end. "Lombardi wanted you exactly 9 feet from the tackle," Knafelc said. "Not 7 feet or 12 feet. It had to be 9 feet. That's how you blocked the linebacker. The pulling guard and the running back would look for the tight end. If they saw his numbers, that meant he had turned the linebacker to the outside, so they went inside. If they didn't see his numbers, that meant he had turned the linebacker to the inside, so they went outside."

The players discovered early that Lombardi was a man of many moods. He could be charming one minute and a tyrant the next. Sometimes he was jovial and gregarious, and other times he was quiet and aloof. When his booming laughter filled the room, the players loved to be around him. But just as often, he walked around with a black cloud over his head. On those days, it was best not to make a mistake on the practice field.

Temp told a story that captured Lombardi's complex personality.

"I'm Catholic and our training camp was at St. Norbert [College]," he said. "We were in a dorm on the south side of the campus, and the chapel was nearby. I'd walk from the dorm to mass in the morning, and Lombardi would also. The masses were at 6:00, 6:30 and 7:00 A.M., and we'd cross paths sometimes. He would be coming from 6:30 mass, and I'd be going to 7:00, or vice versa. One day, he would stop and slap me on the back and say, 'Hiya, Jim! Beautiful day, isn't it?' The next day, he would walk right by me and not look at me and not utter a word.

"He had horrendous mood swings. He would embarrass people. I remember getting on the bus one time to go to practice. Bud Jorgensen was our trainer, and Vince just erupted on him. He was screaming at Bud for some reason. I don't know why. I didn't stick around."

The two things that were sure to set off Lombardi were mental errors and injuries. He had no use for players who made mental mistakes; they simply couldn't play for him. And even though he often had been injured himself as a player at

Fordham University, he had no patience for players who suffered sprained ankles, shin splints, dislocated fingers, or a variety of other "minor" injuries that kept them off the field.

"When he was in one of his moods, he'd walk in the training room and yell, 'What the hell are you all doing in here?' " Temp said. "Everyone would kind of hang their heads, and then we'd all walk out."

As a motivator, however, Lombardi was brilliant. He used every trick in the book to get his players to respond to his leadership, from begging to threatening to acting like a raving lunatic. He seemed to know innately which button to push with each player. Some responded best to his pats on the back, others to verbal abuse.

"Nitschke never would have been Nitschke without Lombardi," Temp said. "Lombardi just intimidated Nitschke so much. He made him a tremendous athlete. He motivated him with intimidation. That worked with Nitschke, but he'd try it with other guys and they'd tell him to go screw himself, and they'd be gone."

"I was one of his ripping boys," Knafelc said. "He screamed at me all the time because I could take it. What else are you going to do? He yelled at Bart one time, and Bart went in to his office and said, 'I can take criticism, but if you want me to lead this ball club, do it one on one. Don't embarrass me in front of the team.' I never heard Lombardi yell at Bart after that.

"There's no doubt he was a great motivator. One of the assistant coaches said Lombardi told him, 'Some coaches might know more than me when it comes to X's and O's, but I have an ability to know what ballplayers can and cannot do.' "

Temp said that near the end of his playing career, he fell out of favor with Lombardi. He thinks it was because he suffered a dislocated shoulder in 1959 and reinjured the shoulder during an exhibition game in 1961. "Back then, a shoulder dislocation was a serious injury for a defensive end or anybody who used two arms," Temp said. "They put a harness on me, but it was difficult to play with because you couldn't raise your arm above shoulder level. And my shoulder popped out a number of times."

Temp eventually underwent surgery in which a tendon was cut and resewed and muscles were rearranged to tighten the shoulder joint. But even those drastic measures didn't prevent him from suffering another injury to the shoulder.

"The doctor suggested I could make a living doing something else, and I said, 'Thank you. I'm a college graduate. I can figure that out,' " said Temp, who turned down offers from the Detroit Lions and San Diego Chargers and went into the insurance business. "To this day," he said, "I can't reach behind and scratch my back with my right arm."

Knafelc played his final season for the Packers in 1962. He then signed with the San Francisco 49ers in order to play a tenth year in the league and be eligible for a bigger pension.

In 1963 it so happened that the Packers played their final game of the season in San Francisco. Knafelc still lived in Green Bay and figured he would save some money if he could fly home with the Packers on their chartered plane.

"Bart and I had been roommates for seven years, so I asked him, 'Do you think Coach Lombardi would let me ride home with you?' " Knafelc said. "Bart said, 'Sure, I don't see why not. Why don't you ask him?' So I called his wife and said, 'Marie, do you think I can fly back with the team?' She said, 'Talk to Coach.' I said, 'No, no, you talk to him.' So she called me back and said, 'Sure, Coach said you can fly with us.' "

Knafelc joined his old teammates at the San Francisco airport, where they promptly found a bar with a television set that was tuned to another NFL game. Now, one of Lombardi's rules was that his players were not allowed to drink at a bar. They could order drinks and take them to tables, but they were not allowed to stand or sit at the bar.

"All the guys were in the bar watching the game," Knafelc said. "Lombardi walked in and everybody started running, and I ran with them. Marie grabbed my arm and said, 'Gary, you don't have to leave.' I said, 'Marie, Coach can still kick me off the plane.' I didn't even play for him, and I was still afraid of him."

On the flight home Lombardi asked Knafelc about his plans, and Knafelc said he intended to retire. "He asked me if I wanted to be the Packers public address announcer," said Knafelc, who still lives in Green Bay, as does Temp. "I started doing that in 1964, and I've been doing it ever since."

Bob Long was drafted by the Packers in the fourth round in 1964. He was a raw but talented wide receiver who had played only one season of college football. Primarily, he had been a basketball player at Wichita State. He stood 6'3", weighed 185 pounds, and had excellent speed and good hands. Physically, he was a prototypical flanker.

The one thing he lacked was experience.

"I only played in seven games in college, but I scored like two touchdowns a game," Long said. "The coach didn't want me to get hurt, so I never really had to block. They had me run 'experimental patterns.' I'd race down the field 40 or 50 yards with two guys covering me.

"Well, after I signed with the Packers, I started getting concerned that I would go to Green Bay and get killed. I walked into my football coach's office at Wichita and said, 'Coach, am I going to have to block at Green Bay?' He said, 'You'd better get ready, because Ray Nitschke is waiting for you.'"

Bob Long (80) scores against the Minnesota Vikings in 1966. Long was overshadowed by such receivers as Max McGee, Boyd Dowler, and Carroll Dale during his four seasons in Green Bay, but he put up impressive numbers despite his modest playing time. (Courtesy Bob Long)

Sure enough, during the first few days of his first NFL training camp, Long found himself in Lombardi's infamous "Nutcracker Drill," in which receivers had to block—or at least try to block—linebackers

"I later found out it was more a test of courage for us," Long said. "Coach Lombardi wanted to see if we would put our heads in there. I'm in line and Max McGee is in front of me. He counts the linebackers across from us and figures out that he's going to have to block Nitschke. So he reaches back and grabs me by the jersey and yanks me in front of him. He says, 'Get up here, rookie.'

"That was an experience. When Nitschke hit you, it was like an explosion. He and [Chicago Bears linebacker Dick] Butkus were the two most emotional players in the league. I tell my kids, 'How would you like to block Nitschke in practice every day and Butkus three times a year in games?' "

Fortunately for Long, Lombardi didn't expect his wide receivers to become great blockers. The Packers running game was so good, Lombardi just asked the receivers to shield off the safeties, or more or less impede them by getting in their way. "When he got mad, he'd call you 'Mister,' " Long said. "He'd say, 'Mister, if you can't block, just get in front of them.' "

Long also had been drafted by the San Diego Chargers of the American Football League. Before he decided to sign with the Packers, he traveled to San Diego to watch the Chargers work out and saw young receivers "leaping all over the field, making great catches." He then asked the Packers to send him a team roster. "I'm looking at the ages of the Packer receivers: Max McGee, 30; Boyd Dowler, 29," Long said. "I said, 'That's the place for me.' That's how I made my decision."

What Long didn't know was that Lombardi was loyal to his veterans and almost never played rookies because their

Late, Great Draft Picks

Vince Lombardi was a shrewd judge of talent, as evidenced by his selections in the National Football League draft. In addition to plucking such players as Tom Moore, Bob Jeter, Herb Adderley, Ron Kostelnik, Tom Brown, Donny Anderson, and Jim Grabowski in the early rounds, Lombardi struck gold in later rounds, too. Among his late-round picks: running back Elijah Pitts, thirteenth round, 1961; tight end Marv Fleming, eleventh round, 1963; and center Ken Bowman, eighth round, 1964. All played key roles on championship teams.

mistakes infuriated him. Furthermore, McGee, Dowler, and Carroll Dale formed one of the best receiving corps in the league.

Long barely got on the field in 1964, catching one pass for 19 yards. But then Dowler got hurt in 1965, and Lombardi moved Long into the starting lineup.

"I started four games in a row and every game I started, I scored a touchdown," Long said. "We won every game. We were down, 21–3, to Detroit at halftime. Lombardi came in our tiny locker room at Tiger Stadium and said, 'Gentlemen, that was the worst exhibition of football I've ever seen. Wait until I get a hold of you on Monday.' Then he turned and walked out. Well, we came out in the third quarter and scored four touchdowns, and we won, 31–21.

"Three weeks later, we played Detroit again, this time in Green Bay. Boyd had been hurt but was getting better. You would think I would play a little. I'm telling you, I didn't get in for one play. Not a single play. After the game [which Green Bay lost, 12–7], some reporter asked Lombardi why Bob Long didn't play. Lombardi looked at him with that scowl and said, 'Bob Long is too young.' That was it. End of conversation."

And so it went for Long. He didn't play much, but when he did, he made the most of his opportunities. He caught 13 passes for 304 yards and 4 touchdowns in 1965, 3 passes for 68 yards in 1966, and 8 passes for 96 yards in 1967.

Lombardi stepped down as head coach after the 1967 season but stayed on as general manager and selected loyal assistant Phil Bengtson to coach the Packers. Most of the team's best players were in their thirties, and Lombardi and Bengtson knew they would have to rebuild the roster. Long was traded to the Atlanta Falcons.

Atlanta's coach was Norb Hecker, who had coached the defensive backs in Green Bay from 1959 to 1965 and had

Follow the Leader

Vince Lombardi hired eleven assistant coaches during his nine years as head coach of the Green Bay Packers. Of those assistants, five went on to become head coaches in the National Football League: Bill Austin (Pittsburgh Steelers, Washington Redskins); Phil Bengtson (Packers); Jerry Burns (Minnesota Vikings); Tom Fears (New Orleans Saints); and Norb Hecker (Atlanta Falcons).

watched Long in practice every day. "I went down to Atlanta, and let me tell you, after practicing against Bob Jeter, Willie Wood, and Herb Adderley every day, running pass patterns against other defensive backs was a piece of cake," Long said. "It was like flag football."

He started for the Falcons and was the talk of the league, catching ten passes in one game and finding the end zone with regularity. "I was having a great year, and lo and behold, [early in] the season, Norb Hecker gets fired," Long said. "Who do they bring in, of all people? Norm Van Brocklin."

Van Brocklin had coached the Minnesota Vikings, who had lost to Lombardi's Packers eleven times in fourteen games since they entered the league in 1961.

"Van Brocklin hated Lombardi, he hated the Packers, he hated anything to do with the Packers," Long said. "The first day of practice under Van Brocklin, I shook off the cornerback, caught the ball, and did everything perfect, but apparently I ran the pattern 2 yards short. Here comes Van Brocklin, shaking his finger at me. He was yelling, 'You're Lombardi's pet! You're Lombardi's pet!' He was cussing at me.

"I didn't know what to say. I just said, 'Thank you very much, Coach. I'll take that as a compliment.' Well, he threw me off the practice field. He let me come back the next day because I was the best receiver he had."

In the fourth game of the season, the Falcons played host to the Packers and lost, 38–7. "We were going to run a sweep, and my job was to crack back against the Packers' linebacker," Long said. "Lee Roy Caffey and Dave Robinson were my friends, and I didn't want to hurt their knee with a block they didn't see coming. So we ran a sweep right, I started coming across the line of scrimmage, and I came toward Lee Roy. As I was coming, I shouted out, 'Lee Roy, watch out.'

"He heard me say that, and he jumped right over me and made the tackle. Well, you can imagine what Van Brocklin said when he watched the film on Monday. He shut down the projector and yelled and screamed. He ran the play back and forth about eight times. To him, I was part of the Lombardi green and gold."

A few weeks later, Long would be involved in a situation that was much more serious than a cussing-out by Van Brocklin. He was driving to the Falcons' offices on a Monday morning when a car traveling in the opposite direction on the freeway jumped the median, went airborne, and slammed into his car head-on. The police figured Long's Pontiac Bonneville was going about fifty miles per hour; the other car was going seventy.

Long, who was alone in his car, had just enough time to react. He pulled his feet up from the floorboard and sprawled across the front seat. The impact compressed the Bonneville's engine block and drove it through the dashboard. Long suffered a broken back, serious internal injuries—including the loss of the use of one of his kidneys—and numerous deep cuts and abrasions. He was in a coma for two weeks. The driver of the other car died in the wreck.

That was the end of Long's season and very nearly the end of his career. In fact he thought about retiring prior to the 1969 season until he got a phone call from one Vincent T. Lombardi, who was now head coach of the Washington Redskins.

Long said, "I got a call: 'Bob Long, this is Coach Vince Lombardi. How are you feeling? How much of a football player are you now, compared to when you were in Green Bay?' I said, 'Probably 80 percent, Coach.' Some of my injuries were healing slowly. He said, 'You probably heard I got named head coach of the Redskins. I need a flanker. I think you might be the guy.' "

Long warned Lombardi that he had lost some foot speed. Lombardi said the Redskins offense was so potent he just needed a tall flanker to catch the ball occasionally.

"I said, 'Look, Coach, the first thing I want you to understand is that I was a pretty good receiver in Green Bay and it was hard for me to get playing time. I will not come to the Redskins if I'm going to sit on your bench. I've had enough of that,' " Long said. "He promised me: 'You will not sit on my bench.' "

Long signed with the Redskins, started at flanker, and caught forty-eight passes in 1969. He also noticed that Lombardi had mellowed a bit. The coach was still emotional and driven and demanding, but his fits of fury were fewer and farther between, and he loosened his tight grasp on every aspect of his players' lives.

"For example, we had a great tight end named Jerry Smith, a great pass catcher," Long said. "Well, he had long hair and Lombardi put up with it. In Green Bay you didn't have long hair. Lombardi was changing with the times a little bit."

The Redskins, perennial losers, went 7–5 in Lombardi's first season. But it was a short-lived honeymoon: In 1970 the great coach died of colon cancer.

"After Lombardi died," Long said, "I kind of lost my spirit for the game."

He retired, but then another old friend, Boyd Dowler, called him and asked him to join the Los Angeles Rams. Dowler had retired himself and now was the Rams' receivers coach. "I said, 'Boyd, don't ask me to come play for you.' " Long said. "He said, 'Bullet, I need you.' So I went there and played five or six games for the Rams. I was the starting flanker, but then I hurt my knee and that was it."

Long is one of few men who played in Madison Square Garden (with Wichita State) and Yankee Stadium (with the

The Best of the Best

Ten men who played for Coach Vince Lombardi in Green Bay are enshrined in the Pro Football Hall of Fame in Canton, Ohio.

They are fullback Jim Taylor (inducted in 1976), tackle Forrest Gregg (1977), quarterback Bart Starr (1977), linebacker Ray Nitschke (1978), cornerback Herb Adderley (1980), defensive end Willie Davis (1981), center Jim Ringo (1981), halfback Paul Hornung (1986), safety Willie Wood (1989), and defensive tackle Henry Jordan (1995).

Lombardi was inducted posthumously in 1971.

Packers), and he is the only man who played for Lombardi in both Green Bay and Washington. Tom Brown and Chuck Mercein also played for Lombardi in Green Bay and signed with the Redskins, but they did not see action in 1969.

Long opened a successful chain of Pizza Hut restaurants and became active in the National Football League Players Association. He helped get pensions for older players who were not grandfathered into the league's pension plan. Although he suffered a stroke in 1991, he continues to work on behalf of retired players.

"I played four years with the Packers, and we won three championships," Long said. "It doesn't get much better than that. My timing was perfect because I couldn't have been with a better team at a better time. I would have played for the Packers for nothing."

Knafelc and Temp feel the same way. They played football in the best of times, when the league was growing and making inroads in television, when fans identified with the players and vice versa, and when the Packers were on top of the world.

They also played for Vince Lombardi.

"I wish I would have had Lombardi the first five years of my career," Knafelc said, "because he made me a better player and a better man."

Lambeau Field Forever

P ackers president Bob Harlan was leaving his office at Lambeau Field one evening during training camp in the mid-1990s when he noticed a van pulling into the parking lot.

On the surface there was nothing unusual about that. The vast expanse of concrete surrounding Lambeau was busy at all hours of the day, with vehicles coming and going: players and coaches reporting to and leaving practice; members of the media, who worked in offices in the bowels of the stadium; public relations staffers and other employees; and fans shopping at the Packer Pro Shop.

But this van had Kansas license plates, so Harlan was curious.

"What caught my attention was the big Kansas Jayhawk decal on the front of the van, because I've got a son who lives there," Harlan said. "I was kind of intrigued by it, so I pulled over to the side and watched.

"A gentleman gets out of the van, he's probably in his early sixties, he's got cameras hanging around his neck, and the first thing he does is get down on his hands and knees and bows three times. Then he kisses the ground. And then the other people get out. There's about four couples, and they've all got cameras."

Lambeau Field, home of the Packers, before luxury suites were added to the rim of the bowl. Lambeau's oval shape, single-deck seating, and unobstructed viewing from every angle make it one of the best places in America to watch a football game. (Vernon J. Biever Photo)

Harlan watched for several minutes as the group slowly walked around the perimeter of Lambeau Field, staring, pointing, talking animatedly, and taking photographs. "It really struck me, how these people had driven all the way from Kansas to see Lambeau Field," Harlan said. "I went into the office the next day and said, 'We just drive by this place every day. We come to work every day and take it for granted. But people just cherish this place.'"

Built by the citizens of Green Bay and put on the map by Vince Lombardi and his Glory Years teams in the 1960s, Lambeau Field is one of the best-known and most revered temples of American sport.

Of the twenty Packers enshrined in the Pro Football Hall of Fame, twelve called Lambeau Field home: Lombardi, Jim Taylor, Forrest Gregg, Bart Starr, Ray Nitschke, Herb Adderley, Willie Davis, Jim Ringo, Paul Hornung, Willie Wood, Henry Jordan, and James Lofton. Furthermore, virtually every NFL superstar since the mid-1950s has played in Lambeau, from Jim Brown and Gale Sayers to Barry Sanders and Walter Payton, from Joe Montana and John Elway to Randy Moss and Michael Vick.

Players love the stadium for its well-maintained grass field and a tradition they swear is palpable. The team's Hall of Fame members are honored on a "Ring of Honor," their names displayed in yellow lettering on the stadium's green walls.

"When visiting teams come in, they have a couple hours before the game starts, and sometimes the players get restless in the locker room," Harlan said. "So you'll see some of them come out with T-shirts on. They'll be on the field talking, just wasting time before they have to start getting ready for the game. But many times you'll see them pointing at the names on the Ring of Honor. You don't see Vince Lombardi's name and not know what happened here. That, to me, adds to the aura of the whole building."

When Ron Wolf was the team's general manager in the 1990s, he often brought free agents to the stadium and walked with them through the tunnel and onto the field. "Ron used to say, 'When I walk out that north end zone and down that ramp and into the stadium, I get goose bumps,' " Harlan said. "He said, 'Every time I bring a free agent to town, I want to walk him down there. I want him to feel what I feel.' "

Fans love Lambeau Field for its easy access and its unobstructed views from virtually every seat. Because the bowl was
built strictly for football, there is no upper deck, and there are
no awkward angles. Even though the stadium is one of the last
to use aluminum bench-type seating, no one complains.

In fact almost everyone who attends a game at Lambeau
Field waxes eloquent about the experience.

"I can't believe there's a fan in any location in the National
Football League — a true football fan — if they had to be honest,
wouldn't say, 'I'd love to go to Lambeau Field at least once,'
Harlan said. "They may hate us. They may be a Bears fan and
hate us. But I can't believe they wouldn't say, 'I'd like to go to
Lambeau Field at least once.' "

Each year, the Packers get dozens of requests from families
of deceased Packers fans to spread the ashes of their loved ones
on the hallowed ground. Regretfully, Harlan said, the team
cannot honor those requests. "We're afraid if we ever started,
the pile of ashes would be pretty high," he said. "We don't want
it to be a tombstone."

Lambeau was built at a cost of $960,000 and dedicated as
City Stadium on September 29, 1957. It was renamed Lambeau
Field in 1965 in honor of legendary Packers coach E. L. "Curly"
Lambeau.

The fact that the stadium was even built reflects the city's
passion for the Packers. The team's best record in the previous
eight seasons had been 6–6, and since 1944 it had finished no
higher than third place in its division. But the Packers, and the
league, had outgrown old City Stadium on the east side of
Green Bay. And when it became apparent that the future of
the franchise hinged on the construction of a new stadium, the
citizens of Green Bay responded. A bond issue received two-to-

Homes, Sweet Homes

The Packers have played home games on eight fields.

In Green Bay they played their earliest home games—from 1919 to 1922—at Hagemeister Park, a sandlot near the East River. Green Bay East High School and Joannes Park now occupy the land.

In the 1923 and 1924 seasons, the Packers played host to teams at Bellevue Park, a minor-league baseball park on North Main Street.

City Stadium, located adjacent to East High School, was the Packers' home from 1925 to 1956. The stadium featured a brick facade and wooden grandstands. It was expanded several times until peak capacity was about 24,500. East High still uses the historic field for its home football games.

On September 29, 1957, the Packers christened new City Stadium with a 21–17 victory over the Chicago Bears. In 1965 the team renamed the stadium Lambeau Field, following the death of Earl L. "Curly" Lambeau, the Packers' cofounder and first coach.

In Milwaukee the Packers played home games at Borchert Field, a minor-league baseball park; State Fair Park on the Wisconsin State Fairgrounds; Marquette Stadium; and Milwaukee County Stadium.

one voter approval in a municipal referendum on April 3, 1956.

Today, Lambeau Field is the oldest continuously occupied stadium in the NFL. The 2003 season marked the Packers' forty-seventh at Lambeau, compared with thirty-seven years for the San Diego Chargers at QUALCOMM Stadium and thirty-two years for the San Francisco 49ers at 3Com Park and the Dallas Cowboys at Texas Stadium.

Only two teams in professional sports have longer continuous home-field tenures than do the Packers: the Boston Red Sox at Fenway Park since 1912 and the Chicago Cubs at Wrigley Field since 1914.

"A couple years ago, we went to New York to play the Giants," Harlan said. "We had a 3:15 P.M. game and some of our people organized a tour of Yankee Stadium. I had never been to Yankee Stadium, so I really wanted to do that. As you're going through it, you think of Ruth and Gehrig and DiMaggio. . . . I felt like a little kid. And I said, 'You know what? This is the way people feel when they come to Lambeau Field.' "

Part of the charm of Lambeau is that, like Wrigley Field, the stadium was built in the middle of a neighborhood. Located at 1265 Lombardi Avenue, a few miles southwest of downtown Green Bay, Lambeau is flanked by modest, neatly kept homes and small businesses. The impressive Don Hutson Center, the team's $4.67 million practice facility, stands just east of the stadium on Oneida Street.

Romanticized by the mellifluous voice of NFL Films narrator John Facenda as the "frozen tundra," and universally recognized as the site of the 1967 NFL Championship Game against the Dallas Cowboys played in subzero temperatures—the famous "Ice Bowl"—Lambeau Field isn't a cold and fore-

The Don Hutson Center, the Packers' state-of-the-art indoor practice facility, was built on the east side of Oneida Street, opposite Lambeau Field. The grass practice field next to the Hutson Center was named in honor of Clarke Hinkle. Hutson, a wide receiver and defensive back, and Hinkle, a fullback, are members of the Pro Football Hall of Fame. (Courtesy Gary D'Amato)

boding place all the time. The weather in September can be quite hot and humid, and October can be pleasant. Snow doesn't generally start flying until December.

"It changes throughout the season," said Tony Mandarich, who played offensive tackle for the Packers from 1989 to 1992. "It's gorgeous in September and October and then in November, it's a sea of orange, with all the fans wearing their hunting clothes. It's kind of hilarious.

"But it's an awesome place to play. There is a lot of tradition there, and you definitely feel it."

That tradition was something Wolf wanted to emphasize and build upon when he was hired by the Packers in 1991. Over the previous six seasons, Green Bay had compiled a pathetic 7–23 record at Lambeau Field. Opponents no longer were fearful of playing on the "frozen tundra." In fact they usually swaggered into Lambeau Field, made fun of the fans, and swaggered out with a victory.

That had to change, if the Packers were ever going to become playoff contenders again.

Wolf hired Mike Holmgren as head coach, and together they stressed the importance of regaining a home-field advantage. They started by building a new Packers team from the turf up. They looked for offensive linemen who were thick and squat, with low centers of gravity so they would stay on their feet when the grass was soft or muddy or buried under snow. They looked for running backs who ran north and south, for receivers who could come out of their cuts without slipping and sliding, for kickers and punters who could handle the elements in December. They lucked out when they traded for quarterback Brett Favre, a Southern boy who seemed oblivious to rain, snow, sleet, ice, howling winds, and numbing cold. It seemed that the worse the conditions were, the better Favre played. Until the Atlanta Falcons upset the Packers in the first round of the 2002 playoffs, Favre had never lost a game at home when the temperature was thirty-four degrees or colder.

In 1994 Packers management made a bold move to enhance the team's home-field advantage. Harlan announced that, beginning with the 1995 season, the Packers would play all their home games at Lambeau Field, eliminating the three regular-season games they had played in Milwaukee County Stadium for years. The announcement upset many Milwaukee fans at the time, but Wolf and Holmgren felt that games at County Stadium were too much like road games because the team had to be bused to Milwaukee and back, a two-hour trip each way.

The move turned out to be a stroke of genius, and the fans in Milwaukee quickly got over whatever resentment they harbored because they were included in a three-game season ticket package at Lambeau . . . and the team was winning.

From 1992 through 2002 the Packers compiled a 67–11 regular-season record at Lambeau, plus a 6–1 record in the playoffs, for an overall home record of 73–12. From 1996 to 2002 they were 61–8 at home (.884), including postseason games.

Green Bay's record at Lambeau Field in December, when the weather turns nasty, was an incredible 18–1 from 1992 to 2002. The Packers outscored their opponents by slightly more than fifteen points per game, or more than a two-touchdown difference, in those games.

"I remember in 1993, we were playing the Raiders [on December 26]," said LeRoy Butler, who played safety for the Packers from 1990 until an injury ended his career in 2001. "It was like twenty-eight below zero with the windchill. I remember watching the news and seeing [Raiders wide receiver] Tim Brown get off the team bus. He was like, 'Man, it's cold here.' When the game started, it looked like they didn't even want to play."

Not surprisingly, Green Bay won, 28–0.

During the Ice Bowl game, Packers defenders knew when the Cowboys were going to run the ball because Dallas wide receiver Bob Hayes kept his hands tucked into his pants at the line of scrimmage.

In addition to the psychological advantage the Packers enjoy at Lambeau Field in cold weather, opponents often have problems with their footing on the turf, which is heated by more than 30 miles of radiant heating pipe buried inches beneath the grass. The pipes were installed in 1997 to replace the original system put in by Lombardi for the 1967 season (and which failed during the Ice Bowl).

"We always had the right stuff to keep warm and we always had the right cleats," Butler said. "Red Batty, the equipment manager, he'd give us the weather report when we got there for the game. He'd say, 'Guys, it's nineteen below zero windchill, here's your stuff. Here's your headgear, here's your thermal underwear, here's your battery-powered socks.' He'd draw it up how it was going to be, and then we wouldn't even think about the weather. We'd just go out and try to kick some butt."

By 2002 Wolf had retired and Holmgren was coaching in Seattle, but their mission to transform Lambeau Field into a den of horrors for opponents had been an unqualified success.

After the league's television contracts, the next-best source of revenue for any team is its stadium. Lambeau was showing signs of age, and in an era of domed multipurpose stadiums and luxury boxes it had dropped to the bottom one-third of the NFL in terms of its ability to produce revenue. It became apparent to Harlan and the team's board of directors in the mid-1990s that the Packers were going to have to address the issue of their outdated stadium, and the sooner the better. Options included tearing down Lambeau Field and building a new stadium on the same site, building on a different site, or renovating the stadium to modernize it and maximize its revenue potential.

After weighing the options, doing feasibility studies, and listening to thousands of fans who wanted to preserve Lambeau for the next generation and beyond, Harlan decided that renovation was the way to go.

"Before we started, we went to South Bend [Indiana] to look at Notre Dame, because that's the closest thing we've got to compare to our bowl," Harlan said. "Notre Dame saved their bowl when they renovated; they just built up around it. And that's where we decided that's exactly what we were going to do.

"The first question we had was about [the structure of] our bowl, because of its age and this climate. How would it hold up? When I was told that it tested very positively, I was thrilled. Because I don't care where you go and what you call it, it's never going to be Lambeau Field again if you have to rebuild.

"First of all, this bowl could never be repeated. The building codes today and the [Americans with Disabilities Act] regulations would never let you build this bowl again. Because of the building codes, the aisles have to be wider, and there has to be more space between the rows. There are just so many things today that would not permit you to build that bowl. So 20,000 of those 56,000 people in the bowl would have gone to an upper deck.

"To go somewhere else and build, the big advantage was you would have had more parking, but it would have never been the same. You could have never created this atmosphere again. It just can't be done."

So the mandate from Harlan to the architects working on the project was to preserve the bowl while modernizing the stadium. "I said, 'Here's what I want: I want a red brick building with green wrought-iron gates. I want it to look like a warehouse. I want this to do for football what Camden Yards [in Baltimore] did for baseball,' " Harlan said.

The facade at the newly renovated Lambeau Field is a combination of red brick and green wrought iron that is intended to capture the style and spirit of ballparks and football stadiums built in the first half of the twentieth century. (Courtesy Gary D'Amato)

Then came the tricky part: selling the $295 million renovation to the citizens of Green Bay and Brown County. Harlan was well aware of how difficult it was for the Milwaukee Brewers to win public approval for a new ballpark to replace County Stadium. Miller Park was built, but only after a titanic struggle for taxpayer support.

Though Green Bay still loved its Packers, the economic and political climates had changed considerably since 1956. "I told people all the time, and I said this during the referendum when we were begging for [the renovation]: 'There are only four of these left. There's Yankee Stadium, Wrigley Field, Fenway Park, and Lambeau Field,' " Harlan said. "When you think about it, every place in this league where great history was made has been torn down and replaced. The example I always give is the Pittsburgh Steelers. The great Steelers teams of the '70s, their place is gone. We can tell our players, 'This is where the Lombardi teams practiced and played. This is where Holmgren's Super Bowl teams practiced and played.' And, to me, that's important."

Harlan played the part of politician to raise support for the referendum. He met with dozens of groups, campaigned through the media, and answered his own phone, taking calls from literally hundreds of fans.

"I think it's just incredible what Bob Harlan did," said Lee Remmel, the team's executive director of public relations. "Let's face it, if Bob wouldn't have put his own personal prestige on the line, this would not have happened. He went door to door, I mean literally door to door, during that referendum. He went out to factories at five-thirty in the morning and shook hands with people coming in and said, 'Please vote yes.' "

The countywide vote on the half-cent sales tax increase was held September 12, 2000, and passed by a narrow margin, 53 percent to 47 percent. The renovation project, jointly financed by the City of Green Bay, Brown County taxpayers, the Packers, and the NFL, was started in 2001 and completed in time for the 2003 season.

When finished, Lambeau Field would be transformed from a stadium used just ten days a year into a year-round fan and tourism destination. The renovation features wider concourses, enhanced concession areas, increased restroom facilities, and a club level for private box and club seat patrons. A new 6,500-square-foot Packers Pro Shop replaces the 1,750-square-foot version.

At the heart of the "new" stadium is Titletown Atrium, which features the Packer Hall of Fame and special event facilities capable of holding everything from small family gatherings and weddings to large social functions and corporate meetings. The Atrium also includes a brewpub, restaurants, and fan interactive areas.

But once fans walk into the bowl—the heart and soul of Lambeau Field—everything looks pretty much the same. The major difference is that the renovation added about 9,600 seats, bringing capacity to 71,500.

"They kept the skeleton the same," Butler said. "They just put more skin on it."

When Harlan was pushing for the renovation, he took repeated calls from an angry fan who blasted the team for not building a state-of-the-art facility with expanded parking. Each time, Harlan listened patiently to the man and explained why he thought it was important to retain as much of the "old" Lambeau Field as possible.

Months later, he took a call from the same fan.

"He said, 'Do you remember me, Bob?' I said, 'No, I don't think I do,' " Harlan said. "He said, 'I gave you hell for eight

In keeping with the theme of honoring tradition at renovated Lambeau Field, the stadium logo—a leather-helmeted quarterback—is a "throwback" dropping back to throw. (Courtesy Gary D'Amato)

months during the referendum. I told you to tear that place down and go someplace else. Get us some parking and put backs on the seats. Build us a nice, big, modern stadium.' And he said, 'I'm calling today to tell you I was wrong. The stadium is beautiful.'

"We've heard that from a lot of people. They say, 'I never dreamed this is what it was going to look like.' And I knew they didn't. I could tell during the referendum that they were skeptical. I worried that it was a dream that was never going to happen. We had this dream, and I wasn't sure we were going to get it. But we did."

Staying for a Spell

The Packers' training camp relationship with St. Norbert College is the longest in NFL history. The Packers began holding their summer training camp at the private college in De Pere, Wisconsin—just a few miles from Lambeau Field—in 1958 and have returned every year since.

Prior to 1958 the Packers held training camps at the University of Wisconsin-Stevens Point (1954–1957); Grand Rapids, Minnesota (1950–1953); and the Rockwood Lodge north of Green Bay (1947–1949).

When future Packers players walk from the locker room out onto football's field of dreams, they will pass over a section of concrete that was saved from the old tunnel. The concrete is surrounded by bricks, and a plaque reminds the players that Packers legends walked over that same concrete on their way to innumerable victories.

Tradition, like paradise, should never be paved.

For Biever, It's All Black and White

It is a stunning game-action photograph, a sliver of football history forever preserved in black and white, an image that captures the efficiency and coordination of the great Green Bay Packers teams under their legendary coach, Vince Lombardi.

In the photograph, taken perhaps three seconds after the ball was snapped, guards Jerry Kramer and Fred "Fuzzy" Thurston are peeling to the right, their helmets swiveled to the left as they look for opposing players to block. Fullback Jim Taylor is carrying the ball, running parallel to Kramer and Thurston, poised to cut up field and "run to daylight," as Lombardi would say.

Quarterback Bart Starr is circling back to the left, having handed the ball to Taylor a second earlier. And in the background, framed perfectly between Taylor and Starr, is the great man himself, Lombardi, standing on the sideline in his trademark trench coat and fedora, watching his moving masterpiece: the Packer sweep.

The date was October 22, 1961. The place was Metropolitan Stadium, home of the Minnesota Vikings, the National Football League's newest franchise. The Packers would win that game, the first in what has become one of pro football's most intense rivalries, 33–7. They were on their way to their first of five championships under Lombardi.

If a still photograph can convey athletic poetry in motion, this is it. The photo doesn't just say 1,000 words, it says 10,000. More than four decades later, it still touches the heart and soul of Packers fans who remember that team, that time, and that signature shining excellence.

A copy of the photograph hangs in Vernon Biever's office in the back of the travel agency he owns in Port Washington, Wisconsin.

The Packer sweep was all but unstoppable. Guards Jerry Kramer (64) and Fuzzy Thurston (63) pulled around the end to block, and fullback Jim Taylor (31) followed them and then "ran to daylight." In this famous photo quarterback Bart Starr (15) has handed off to Taylor; in the background, framed between Starr and Taylor, Lombardi watches the play unfold. (Vernon J. Biever Photo)

And well it should. He is the man who took it.

"That was made in 1961, with a single-lens reflex camera but no motor [drive]," Biever said. "Without having a motor and shooting that way, you had to pretty much guide yourself as to when you click the shutter. Timing is everything, and you want to get it at just the peak moment. I think that sort of helped me anticipate the critical time to snap the shutter. Whereas nowadays, with motor drives, you're [shooting] way before and way after and hoping something in between is okay.

"What makes that picture is Lombardi across the way, between Starr and Taylor. Lombardi is standing on the sideline like it's a posed picture. That's without a motor drive. That's more luck than sense, you know?"

Biever is just being modest. It's a wonderful photograph, taken by one of the great sports photographers of all time. Some of Vernon Biever's pictures are hanging in the Pro Football Hall of Fame in Canton, Ohio. He is a *member* of the Packers Hall of Fame.

Biever has been the Packers' team photographer for more than fifty years. Born May 21, 1923, he was a young man when he shot photos of Packers cofounder Curly Lambeau on the sideline in the 1940s. He was forty-four when Lombardi's Packers won their third straight NFL championship in 1967. He was seventy when the team started winning again in the early 1990s under General Manager Ron Wolf and Coach Mike Holmgren.

He has chronicled six NFL championship teams and the careers of nineteen members of the Pro Football Hall of Fame, from Don Hutson and Tony Canadeo to Starr and Taylor and Ray Nitschke.

"I'm a lucky guy," Biever said.

He was fresh out of Port Washington High School in the

summer of 1941 when he walked into the sports editor's office at the *Milwaukee Sentinel* and offered to cover the Packers for the newspaper, which didn't send its own photographer to games in those days. Much to Biever's surprise, the sports editor agreed to give him a chance.

His first assignment was a game against the Chicago Bears at old City Stadium, behind Green Bay East High School. The next day, his photos, shot with an old, clumsy Speed Graphic camera, appeared in the *Milwaukee Sentinel*, and the paper hired him to work the rest of the team's home games that season.

The next year, Biever left St. Norbert College in De Pere, Wisconsin, for World War II. He had enlisted and wound up in the Army's 100th Infantry Division, which had its own newspaper. Biever went to work for the paper and shot photos throughout the European theater.

He returned to St. Norbert College after the war, but by then the *Milwaukee Sentinel* was staffing Packers games with its own photographers. Undeterred, Biever approached the Packers with the idea of becoming the team's official photographer. It was a good deal for the Packers: They would supply him with a sideline pass, and he would supply them with photographs. "I was doing it out of my own pocket," he said. "I enjoyed the photography part, and I enjoyed pro football."

Every spring, Biever packed a suitcase full of negatives, photos, and slides and headed for New York City, where he made cold calls at the offices of public relations firms and book and magazine publishers. "I would tell them I had some pretty good stuff on the Green Bay Packers," he said. "Oh, I was a salesman."

Green Bay was a moribund franchise throughout the 1950s, but the team made a remarkable about-face in 1959 under its first-year coach, an emotional Italian-American named Vince Lombardi. It was the beginning of a new era in the small northern outpost that would soon be nicknamed "Titletown, U.S.A." It also was the beginning of a new era for the team's official photographer.

By the mid-1960s, photographs of Lombardi and the Packers were in demand by the publishers of those football and sports magazines in New York. Biever stopped making his annual spring trips, and people started calling him. For the first time the money Biever made from selling copies of his photographs covered his expenses.

Biever recalls the 1960s with great fondness. Long before the days of digital photography, he used a single-lens reflex Nikon camera to capture some of the greatest images in NFL history, all in black and white. "The single-lens reflex camera became popular in the 1960s, and that changed everything," he said. "Before that, you had to prefocus on the field, maybe the first chalk line or something, and wait until the action got there. If I were to take six or eight pictures a game, that would be a lot. Ten would be exceptional."

As the official team photographer, Biever had unrestricted access along the sideline and was welcomed in the Packers' postgame locker room (he stayed out after losses). Some of his best work of the 1960s includes vivid portraits of such stars as Hall of Famers Forrest Gregg, Paul Hornung, and Starr.

Biever also snapped most of the memorable shots of Lombardi, although the volatile and intimidating coach at first was an uncooperative subject. "Vince Lombardi did not like to have his picture taken," Biever said. "In the beginning, boy, I tell you, I had to stand between a couple players and edge out every so often. If he spotted me, he'd glare at me, and I'd almost shrink. But after a while, he mellowed. In fact I talked to his wife one time, and she said, 'He likes your pictures.' "

Once, after Biever took a posed photograph of Lombardi and one of his friends standing on the field, the coach sent him a letter of thanks. It was typed by Lombardi's secretary and began, "Dear Mr. Biever," But Lombardi crossed out those words with a pen and wrote, simply, "Vern." He signed the letter, which hangs in Biever's office, along with dozens of other breathtaking photos, many of them personalized and signed over the years by grateful Packers.

Biever spent so much time around Lombardi's Packers and watched so many games from the sideline, that he might as well have been inside their huddle. More often than not, he guessed correctly which play Starr was going to call, and that knowledge helped him get shots others missed. "I could pretty much stand where I knew the action was going to be," he said.

He is particularly proud of his shot of a beaming Lombardi receiving the trophy that eventually would be named after him from NFL Commissioner Pete Rozelle after the Packers beat the Kansas City Chiefs, 35–10, in Super Bowl I (then called the AFL–NFL Championship Game).

"I haven't seen another picture of that moment," he said. "I think NFL Films was there, but I might have been the only still photographer. If you're talking about history, that picture is pretty important."

Biever didn't miss many shots during the Lombardi era, but one that he did miss ranks among the most memorable sports photographs of all time. It was taken by Biever's son, John, then just sixteen years old. If you follow pro football at all, you've seen the photo: Starr scoring the game-winning touchdown against the Dallas Cowboys in the famous 1967 "Ice Bowl" game.

"John was trailing along that day," Biever said. "He had no cameras, so I gave him one. He was a very good photographer in high school, but he used my stuff because he had no cameras. So I took along an extra camera that day."

To set the scene, the Packers had won NFL titles in 1965 and 1966 and were trying to become the first team in league history to win three consecutive championships. They played host to the Dallas Cowboys on December 31, 1967. The winner would go on to play the American Football League champion in Super Bowl II.

The temperature at Lambeau Field at game time was a bone-chilling thirteen degrees below zero, and the windchill was minus forty-six. The Packers trailed, 17–14, when they got the ball with 4:50 left in the game and began what is now considered one of the greatest drives in football history. Behind Starr and the hard running of unheralded halfback Chuck Mercein, the Packers wound up at the Cowboys' 1 yard line with thirteen seconds remaining.

Vern and John Biever found themselves standing together just behind the end zone. They decided to separate before the final play so they wouldn't take duplicate photos, although neither remembers who first made the suggestion.

"I don't know if it was his idea or mine," said John Biever, now a staff photographer for *Sports Illustrated*, with more than one hundred cover shots to his credit. "I think I said, 'Maybe we should split up because there are two stories here. There's the play itself, and there's Lombardi's reaction to the play.' "

This is how Vern remembered it: "I said, 'John, we're going to be in different places, because there's no sense getting two pictures that are the same.' He had a 135 millimeter lens, so I said, 'John, you stay right here. This is the right lens for you.' I looked over at the Packers bench, and I said, 'If somebody should score, maybe Lombardi will show some emotion.' Well, Starr did score, and Lombardi turned and ran off the field,

Sixteen-year-old John Biever captured one of the most important moments in Packers history on a single-frame Nikon when most motorized cameras had stopped working in the subzero chill of the "Ice Bowl." Bart Starr (15) crosses the goal line on a quarterback sneak to lift the Packers to a 21–17 victory in the 1967 National Football League championship game at Lambeau Field. (John Biever Photo)

along with the team. I got some very good pictures of his back."

And John?

"He got the picture of the century," Vern said with a laugh.

John Biever's photo, taken with a single-frame Nikon camera—most of the motorized cameras had stopped working in the subzero chill—is one of the most reproduced sports images of all time. Starr is on the ground under a pile of players, having followed the blocks of center Ken Bowman and guard Jerry Kramer into the end zone. Mercein is riding the crest of the pile, his arms raised in the air. Most people who view the photo mistakenly believe Mercein was signaling "touchdown." Instead, he was demonstrating to the officials that he had not helped push Starr into the end zone, which would have resulted in a penalty.

"At that point you're so cold and numb, you hope you're getting the shot," John Biever said. "A lot of times when you get a picture, it kind of registers in your mind. You say to your-self, 'I think I got that one.' This one, I don't remember having that thought. I guess I didn't know for sure that I had it."

He had it, all right. Vern Biever estimated he has sold several hundred copies of the famous photograph.

"Absolutely," John agreed. "Maybe several thousand. I see it everywhere. We'll see the photo on a plaque or something and I'll ask my dad, 'Did you sell this one?' And he'll say, 'No, did you?' It's everywhere."

Vern Biever continued to shoot the Packers through the lean years of the 1970s and 1980s. He reluctantly made the transition from black and white to color film. He traveled with the team on its chartered flights to road games for nearly thirty years. "I don't do that anymore," he said. "For one thing you're flying out of Green Bay, and then I have to drive home [to Port Washington, about 90 miles]. We always come home right after the game is played. I've done it already where I've covered a Monday night game in San Diego, flew back to Green Bay, and drove home. Sometimes, I've seen the sun come up.

"I've been there, done that. It's just way too much for me, at my age."

The Green Bay Packers' first family of photography: Vernon J. Biever (center) with sons John (left) and Jim at Super Bowl XXXV. Biever and his sons have shot tens of thousands of pictures of the Packers, some of which are on display at the Pro Football Hall of Fame in Canton, Ohio. (Vernon J. Biever Photo)

Since the early 1990s, Biever has shared official team photography duties with another son, Jim. Going into the 2004 season, Vern planned to attend all the home games, as has been his custom for more than fifty years. Jim travels with the team to road games.

Another concession Biever has made to age is that he stopped going to the Super Bowl . . . after the first thirty-five. He was one of only a handful of photographers to shoot every Super Bowl game, but the streak ended with Super Bowl XXXVI, in 2002.

"My credentials are still in the drawer," Biever said with a wistful smile. "I made up my mind [not to go] at the last moment. Security. Long lines. I'm not going to do it. It was just too much for me. So I called the NFL and said, 'Cancel me, I'm not coming.' The guy said, 'That's too bad.' A day or two before the game, a big box is delivered in my breezeway by Federal Express. The game program, a press pin, all kinds of things. Very, very nice. I really appreciated that.

"It was hard to miss the first one, it really was. I had to watch it on TV and, boy, it was tough, because I'd recognize where I would be on this play or that play, you know? Missing the camaraderie . . . that's what I really missed. The game itself was an afterthought."

Biever's eyes aren't quite as sharp as they once were. He has had cataract surgery, which didn't help, and laser surgery, which also didn't help much. He has trouble reading the news-paper, but on the field it's another story, because telephoto lenses still get him inside a player's face mask from 80 yards.

An assistant helps carry Biever's cameras and lenses, and his bag still is loaded with pretty much the same equipment he used in the 1960s. Most photographers have switched to digital cameras because of the instantaneous demands of the Internet, but the digital equipment is expensive, and Biever figures he's too old to change. The way he looks at it, switching from the clunky Speed Graphic camera to the single-lens reflex was enough change in one man's life.

Biever commands so much respect that he is one of few photographers who are allowed to stand during Packers games; most are required to kneel to avoid obstructing the view of others. "He's one of the few who doesn't get hassled," said Jim Biever. "I think he's earned that respect . . . or maybe they're afraid of him, I don't know. The photographers in Green Bay make room for him or get out of his way.

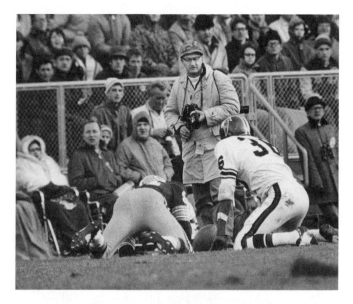

As the Packers' official team photographer, Vernon J. Biever acquired a knack for being in the right place at the right time. His contributions to the team's rich history earned him a place in the Packers Hall of Fame. (Vernon J. Biever Photo)

"When he used to go to the Super Bowl, photographers along the sideline were asking for his autograph. He's got a cult of followers."

In all his years of shooting pro football, Biever has been run over by a player just once on the sideline, during a game against the Bears at Wrigley Field years ago. "The field actually was a little bit muddy," Biever said. "Bart had to drop back into the end zone to pass. There was a safety blitz on him, and one of our backfield guys blocked this one Bears player coming in, and he continued on and pushed me over. The Bears guy came over and picked me up. I always say if he knew I was the Packers photographer, I'd still be laying there."

More recently, Packers quarterback Brett Favre nearly collided with Biever on a scramble out of bounds. "He was running back onto the field, and he said, 'Careful, Vern. You gotta move a little faster,'" Biever said with a laugh.

Although he is old enough to be Favre's grandfather, Biever considers the quarterback to be a good friend. Favre hired Biever to be his wedding photographer when he married his wife, Deanna, and Biever also has taken portraits that the Favre family has used on its Christmas cards.

The crowning achievement of Biever's illustrious career occurred when he was inducted into the Packers Hall of Fame as a contributor in July 2002. He went in with wide receiver Sterling Sharpe.

"No way did I ever think I would get into the Hall of Fame in Green Bay," Biever said. "I had one big supporter. One big, huge supporter that took me in there: Bart Starr. He has some influence, although he tried to get me in the year before, and I didn't make it.

"I saw him in March [2002] at a dinner in Milwaukee. He said, 'This year, I am making it a point. There is no question about it. You are going to be in the Hall of Fame.' I found out later he had written a letter to all the members of the selection committee and he had, in fact, called some. And, of course, it happened."

Starr presented Biever at the induction ceremony. Packers coach Mike Sherman made it a point to personally congratulate the photographer. The theme of Biever's speech that night was that he was a lucky man, a man who appreciated all that the Packers had done for him.

The Packers also are fortunate. Had it not been for Biever, a very big and very important part of the franchise's story would be incomplete.

Like all great photographers, he was in the right place at the right time.

Lombardi Avenue, Memory Lane

F uzzy Thurston's #63, the bar Thurston owns on West Mason Street in Green Bay, not far from Lambeau Field, is filled with memorabilia and paraphernalia from his football career. The walls are crowded with so many plaques, paintings, banners, and photographs that the place could pass for a sort of Hall of Fame with pool tables.

Frederick "Fuzzy" Thurston is everywhere on those walls. He is in photographs with Coach Vince Lombardi, with running back Paul Hornung, with quarterback Bart Starr. Many of the photos and paintings depict, in various incarnations, the Packers sweep. It was Lombardi's bread-and-butter play, and it was the play that gave Thurston his identity and his enduring fame and popularity in Wisconsin.

There's Fuzzy, leading Elijah Pitts around the corner in a grainy black and white. There's Fuzzy, with Hornung in tow in a classic shot. There's Fuzzy and Jerry Kramer, leading Jim Taylor in a beautiful lithograph. Frozen moments of perfection.

But the photograph that reveals the most about Thurston hangs in an out-of-the-way corner of the bar. In it, Fuzzy is staring into the camera, a huge cigar clenched in a cat-that-ate-the-canary grin. Taylor and Kramer are in the photo, too, but they're too busy celebrating another Packers victory to notice the photographer.

Not Fuzzy. His eyes full of life, his smile incandescent, he mugs for the camera. The photograph says that Thurston has led a charmed life, and that he knows it. But that is not to say he has lived a life free from pain and suffering and sadness.

Thurston lost his father when he was four, lost his shirt in the late 1970s when his eleven Left Guard Steak House restaurants went under, lost his larynx to cancer shortly after that, and lost both hips to replacement surgery in 1992.

On the plus side of the ledger, he played nine seasons for Vince Lombardi.

"We came to Green Bay together [in 1959], and we went out together [after Super Bowl II]," Thurston said. "That's always my claim to fame. Every day, I thank God that I've had the opportunity to be a Wisconsin native, a former Packer, and a Packers fan."

When Thurston talks, he has to exert pressure on an artificial voice box and control his breathing to produce speech. His "voice" is a hoarse whisper, and in a loud room, you have to lean close to hear it. Yet, wherever he goes, Fuzzy Thurston is the life of the party. When the glory years faded and the team's superstars scattered, Fuzzy stayed behind. He and linebacker Ray Nitschke, who also made his permanent home in Green Bay, were the team's most popular retired players. Nitschke died of a heart attack on March 8, 1998, and Fuzzy inherited the unofficial title of franchise ambassador.

It's a role he clearly cherishes.

His bar is a mecca for Packers fans looking to cling to a warm memory. Thurston spends a good deal of time at the bar—especially on the weekends when the Packers play at home—where he poses for pictures, signs autographs, and tells stories. Outgoing, charming, with a handsome, toothy smile, he mingles with the patrons, shaking hands and slapping backs. Sometimes, he startles them by grabbing them in a bear hug and rasping "I love you" in their ears.

During player introductions at the annual Packers Alumni Game, Thurston always gets one of the loudest ovations as he charges onto the field.

His statewide popularity was never more evident than when voting for the Wisconsin Athletic Hall of Fame was opened to the public in 2003. Fans got to select one person for induction, and Thurston was the people's choice. He edged more than a dozen prominent nominees, including former Milwaukee Bucks star Kareem Abdul-Jabbar, former Packers Reggie White and Sterling Sharpe, state basketball coaching legend Dick Bennett, and former Milwaukee Brewers star Cecil Cooper.

Thurston was inducted into the Hall on June 12, 2003.

"That was the best," he said. "I've always said that the smartest and most knowledgeable fans in the world are Green Bay Packers fans. I've been in the bar business a long time. I've had beers with them. I've eaten hamburgers with them. I've signed autographs for them. More people have met me than any other Packer from that team. To get in that Hall of Fame the way I did was the greatest thrill I've ever had. It was a very special night."

Thurston also is a member of the Green Bay Packers Hall of Fame (inducted in 1975), the Valparaiso Athletic Hall of Fame, the Indiana Athletic Hall of Fame, and the Wisconsin College Coaches Association Hall of Fame.

He is not among the ten players from Lombardi's teams who have joined their coach in the Pro Football Hall of Fame in Canton, Ohio. But then, Dave Robinson, Ron Kramer, Max McGee, and Boyd Dowler are not there, either, and a strong case for induction could be made for each.

Success Breeds Success

Six players who donned the green and gold
at some point in their careers were named
to the National Football League's Seventy-
Fifth Anniversary Team in 1994: tackle Forrest
Gregg; linebackers Ray Nitschke and Ted
Hendricks; end Don Hutson; defensive end
Reggie White; and placekicker Jan Stenerud. In
addition, Hutson, Clarke Hinkle, and Cal Hubbard
were named to the NFL's all-time Two-Way Team.

"[Bob] Skoronski was as good as Forrest Gregg," Thurston said of Lombardi's starting offensive tackles. Gregg is in the Hall of Fame; Skoronski is not. "We could have fifteen or sixteen players in there, easy. But they're not going to put that many in."

No matter. Thurston played for five world championship teams in Green Bay, and that's good enough for him. "There's nothing in the world like winning to make people be happy and work hard," he said, pointing to a team photograph from the 1960s. "We were thirty guys who loved each other. We were brothers. We didn't want to let the other guy down. We didn't make mistakes because we were always thinking of the guy next to us.

"I thank God every day. I played on the greatest football team the game has ever seen."

As one of eight children growing up fatherless in Altoona, Wisconsin, a tiny town near the Mississippi River, Thurston never entertained dreams of becoming a professional athlete.

His imagination stretched only so far. He hoped to someday make it to a basketball or football game at the University of Wisconsin. He didn't think about *playing* at Wisconsin; he just wanted to sit in the stands. He knew very little about the Green Bay Packers, because National Football League games were not yet televised. To a young boy growing up in Altoona in the 1930s and 1940s, Green Bay might as well have been Shanghai.

Thurston didn't play high school football because Altoona High School didn't have a football team. There were sixteen kids in his graduating class. He was the only member of the school's track team, competing in the shot put and discus and also running the 100-yard dash. He also played basketball, and played it well enough to earn a scholarship to Valparaiso University in Indiana.

He was the only child in the Thurston family to graduate from high school.

At Valparaiso Thurston was a ruggedly built 6-foot guard who started occasionally but mostly came off the bench. He weighed 185 pounds but was bull-chested, strong, and athletic, if not graceful.

During his sophomore year Valparaiso's football coach approached him. "He said, 'Fuzzy, you're in the wrong sport. You should be playing football, but you've got to get bigger,'" Thurston said. "He got me a job in an icehouse, and I put on thirty-five pounds that summer. All muscle. I went out for the team and weighed 225 pounds. The next year, I weighed 235. I still had a semester of eligibility left, and he talked me into coming back for a third year. I'm glad he did because by then I knew what I was doing. I was the most valuable player in the conference."

The Philadelphia Eagles selected Thurston in the fourth round of the 1956 NFL draft. He was a 250-pound guard, green as grass but tough as nails, with a square jaw and a buzz haircut and a nonstop motor. He was intense and determined but lacking a bit in technique and talent. "I tried to get a $500 signing bonus from the Eagles, but they said, 'Absolutely not,'" Thurston said with a laugh. "Can you imagine that? They said, 'We'll tell you what we're going to do. If you don't make the team, we'll pay for your flight home.'"

A few weeks later, he was on a flight home. The Eagles had released him.

Before he could catch on with another team, the army called. When Thurston finished his hitch, the Chicago Bears' coach, George Halas, signed him to a contract. Within days after Thurston reported to training camp in 1958, Halas traded

A Weighty Issue

Fuzzy Thurston played at about 260 pounds during his prime with the Packers. Nowadays, it's unusual to find a starting guard in the National Football League who weighs less than 290. Year-round weight-training and the use of supplements—and in some cases, banned steroids—account for much of the extra bulk on players today. Thurston believes the extra weight is at least partly responsible for the high incidence of injuries among offensive linemen.

him back to the Eagles, who released him again, this time before the first game of the season.

Bud Grant, who would later coach the Minnesota Vikings, was then the head coach of the Winnipeg franchise in the Canadian Football League. He called and offered a job to Thurston. Fuzzy got in his car and drove straight to Canada.

After just ten days in Winnipeg, Grant called him into his office. "He said, 'The Baltimore Colts want you. I think you should go,' " Thurston said. "So I got in my car and drove to Baltimore. I wasn't really frustrated because I knew I could play. I knew I was going to play somewhere."

Thurston made the Colts roster and wound up playing in the 1958 NFL title game — the famous sudden-death overtime game in which the Colts defeated the New York Giants, 23–17. That game, played during television's infancy, often is referred to as the game that put the NFL on the map.

"I played special teams and made an important tackle," Thurston said. "I contributed to that victory. I got a world championship ring. I finally had a good job."

Or, at least, he thought he had a good job.

During the early days of training camp in 1959, Thurston was informed that he had been traded to the Green Bay Packers. "I had mixed feelings," he said. "Green Bay was 1–10–1 the year before. They were a bad team. I had never even been to Green Bay, but it was like going home."

On his way to Green Bay, Thurston stopped at his home in Madison, Wisconsin, to visit with his wife, Susan, who had just given birth to the couple's second son. He stayed overnight and reported to the Packers the next day.

"Lombardi walked up to me in the locker room and said, 'Who the hell are you?' " Thurston said. "That was the first

Fuzzy Thurston (63) looks for an opponent to block as Paul Hornung (5) prepares to throw a pass. Thurston, the team's steady left guard, timed his career perfectly, joining the team during Vince Lombardi's first year as coach and retiring after Lombardi's last year as coach. (Vernon J. Biever Photo)

time I had ever seen him. I said, 'I'm Fuzzy Thurston.' He said, 'You're late,' and he walked away. He had expected me to be there the day before. I knew I would never be late again."

Thurston won the starting job at left guard. Kramer was the right guard, and they would be in the lineup together, leading the sweep, for the next nine years. "In order for the sweep to go, you have to have two very quick guards, a very quick center, a great tight end, a great blocking back, and a great running back," Thurston said. "We had it all. That was the first play Lombardi ever diagrammed, and we ran it thirty times a day in practice.

"He said, 'If this goes, they cannot stop the rest.' So we had to make it go."

That they did. For the better part of a decade, the sweep was all but unstoppable. Every defense knew it was coming, and no defense could shut it down. Just as Lombardi had said, the sweep made the other plays work. The Packers didn't pass often, but when they did, receivers were open and Starr got them the ball. The entire offense was predicated on teamwork and timing—and it all started with the sweep.

For the first time in NFL history, people other than opposing scouts were paying attention to the offensive linemen. Thurston and Kramer became symbols of the sweep because they were out in front as they pulled either right or left in tandem, numbers 63 and 64, flattening linebackers and safeties who got in their way.

They were very good at their jobs.

"Before the Lombardi sweep, nobody knew the difference between the guards, the tackles, and the center," Thurston said. "They were just offensive linemen."

Kramer and Thurston, two men who never shied away from publicity, basked in the spotlight. "There are two good reasons the Packers are world champions," Thurston would say when he spoke at banquets. "Jerry Kramer is one of them, and you're looking at the other."

In a rare public display of appreciation for the individual player, Lombardi once said that Kramer was the best guard in the league and one of the greatest in NFL history. "Fred Thurston," he continued, "is a man of extraordinary determination and pride. He makes the difference between an average athlete and a good one."

The Packers enjoyed one of the greatest runs in NFL history. They won league championships in 1961, 1962, 1965, 1966, and 1967. They also won Super Bowls I and II, but Thurston is still bothered by the fact that fans seem to put more emphasis on Super Bowl titles than they do the pre–Super Bowl designation as "world champions."

"All people talk about is the Super Bowl," he said. "It's like the NFL started in 1967 and nobody won titles before that. There were a lot of great teams in the 1940s, '50s, and '60s that don't get much recognition."

After the 1967 season, Lombardi ran into Thurston at a banquet, sized him up and growled, "When are you going to retire?" Thurston got the message. He had no desire to play out

Starting a Tradition

The starting offense for the Green Bay Packers in Super Bowl I consisted of Carroll Dale at left end, Bob Skoronski at left tackle, Fuzzy Thurston at left guard, Bill Curry at center, Jerry Kramer at right guard, Forrest Gregg at right tackle, Marv Fleming at tight end, Bart Starr at quarterback, Elijah Pitts at halfback, Jim Taylor at fullback, and Boyd Dowler at split end.

the string for another team, not after playing for Lombardi and the Packers. So he retired.

Thurston went into the restaurant business, but the chain expanded too quickly and he eventually had to close his Left Guard Steak Houses. He beat cancer in 1980, though it cost him his voice. Twelve years later, he had his hips replaced. "I always say that if you run the sweep as much as Jerry and I did, you'll wind up with new hips someday," he said. "I don't know why Jerry doesn't have them yet. But I guess he's a couple years younger than me."

Though his playing career ended more than thirty-five years ago, Thurston remains one of the team's biggest and most visible fans. He has missed just two home games since he retired, once when he was hospitalized with cancer and once when he attended an uncle's funeral. "It's so much fun to watch Brett [Favre]," he said of the Packers' future Hall of Fame quarterback. "For me to have played with Bart and to be able to watch Brett . . . that's a lot of years of great quarter-backing."

Times are changing in Green Bay and in the National Football League. The most money Thurston ever made in one year during his playing days was $27,500. Many players in the league make one hundred times that amount today.

But Thurston doesn't yearn for the "good old days." He likes to talk about the 1960s, but he doesn't live in the past. He is glad to see the sport and the team progress, secure in the knowledge that he played an important role on the NFL's best team during a period of unprecedented growth for the league.

One summer day in 2003, a few months before the newly renovated Lambeau Field would be unveiled during the regular season, Thurston wandered into the massive glass-

Fuzzy Thurston celebrates in the Louisiana Superdome press box during the final moments of the Packers 35–21 victory over the New England Patriots in Super Bowl XXXI. Thurston, whose playing career ended in 1967, remains one of the team's biggest fans. (Courtesy Gary D'Amato)

walled atrium and looked around. He couldn't believe what he saw. "I was all by myself," he said, "and I started crying. I might be going overboard, but if we wouldn't have had the success we had in the '60s, I don't think we would have a new stadium today."

If you walked into Fuzzy's #63 on a busy night and surveyed the patrons, it would be difficult to find a single person who disagreed.

The Quintessential Packer

Odds are that unless you're a die-hard fan of the Green Bay Packers, you've never heard of Lee Remmel or Art Daley. Neither man played a single down for the Packers or coached the team in any capacity. Yet their association with the franchise goes back to the 1940s, and few men, if any, can claim to have attended more Packers games, at home or on the road.

Remmel, who was born June 20, 1924, was a sportswriter and columnist for the *Green Bay Press-Gazette* for nearly thirty years before joining the Packers as director of public relations in 1974. Since 1989 he has been the team's executive director of public relations, with responsibility for overseeing public relations, marketing, and community relations.

Through 2003 he had attended all thirty-seven Super Bowl games, the first eight as a reporter for the *Press-Gazette* and the rest as a member of the National Football League's auxiliary media relations staff (except Super Bowls XXXI and XXXII, in which the Packers played and Remmel attended with the team's front office).

Incredibly, Remmel has attended more than one hundred Packers–Bears games and every game the Packers have played against the Minnesota Vikings, who joined the NFL in 1961.

On March 30, 1996, Remmel was inducted into the Green Bay Packer Hall of Fame. "Lee Remmel has played an important role in National Football League history," said NFL Commissioner Paul Tagliabue. "From the 1940s Lee has spent his career informing Packers fans about their team. The NFL serves more fans than any other sport, and Lee has served Packers fans longer than anyone else in club history. His tremendous depth of Packers knowledge is immensely valuable to both the club and the league. The Packers are a vital part of the NFL tradition, and no one is more synonymous with the Packers than Lee Remmel."

Daley, who was born August 15, 1916, started working for the *Press-Gazette* in 1941. He served his country during World War II then rejoined the newspaper in 1946. He was named sports editor and worked side by side with Remmel until 1967, when Daley became the paper's telegraph editor.

Daley retired in 1978 but continues to write a column for *Packer Report*, the team's official publication. He has done so since the publication was launched in 1973. He was a longtime member of the Pro Football Hall of Fame selection committee, and he still attends every Packers home game.

Over lunch at Kroll's, a family-style restaurant and Green Bay institution on Ridge Road, just across the street from Lambeau Field, Remmel and Daley talked about their long association with the franchise.

Their memories were sharp, their wit quick, and the stories came tumbling out—stories that span seven decades and hundreds of games. They have seen it all, these two, from the leather-helmet days to the era of domed stadiums and luxury boxes, from Curly Lambeau to Brett Favre.

Here are excerpts from our conversation:

On Curly Lambeau, the Packers' cofounder and first coach

Remmel: "What do you want to know about Curly? Do you want to know the truth? He was a flamboyant man and a good coach. He won more than 200 games. You can't do that with mirrors. He won six NFL championships."

Daley: "He was thirty-one years old when he won his first championship. He was born in 1898."

Remmel: "He was twenty-one when he launched the team. One thing that struck me about Curly, as a starry-eyed kid— you have to realize I was a young guy then, and so was Art, and Lambeau was already a legitimate legend—was that he was always supremely confident."

Daley: "That was his long suit. I always called him an incurable optimist. That's the way he was. He never thought he would lose a game."

Remmel: "And he didn't lose many until the very end. He was 6–5 in '46 and he was 6–5–1 in '47. Then the last two years, he was 3–9 and 2–10. One thing he did early in the 1949 season, as Art remembers very well, he kicked himself upstairs after the Bears beat the hell out of them in the first game. It was 17–0. Curly kicked himself upstairs and called himself the 'advisory coach.' You have to realize he was the vice president, general manager, and head coach. He could do whatever he wanted. He *was* the Green Bay Packers."

Daley: "If it wasn't for him, there wouldn't be any of this. There would be nothing."

Remmel: "That's one thing that kind of irritates me. You have to give Vince Lombardi full credit for what he did. But if it wouldn't have been for Curly Lambeau, there would have been no Vince Lombardi in Green Bay. There would have been no team, no stadium, no franchise."

Art Daley (left), Richard "Red" Smith (center), and Earl Gillespie hit the airwaves to talk about the Green Bay Packers. Smith served as an assistant coach to Curly Lambeau from 1935 to 1943. Gillespie was one of Wisconsin's best-known radio and television personalities. (Courtesy Art Daley)

On their early years in journalism and covering the Packers in the days of typewriters and train travel

Remmel: "Early in my career, I covered two murders in three days in Shawano County. A woman took her son out to a chopping block and chopped off his head. The next day, she was committed to the state hospital for the criminally insane. The day after that, a guy held up a bank in western Shawano County. The cashier followed him out of the bank—he was warned not to—and the bank robber shot him right between the eyeballs. Talk about frontier justice. That happened about noon. By eight o'clock that night, a posse had been formed, he had been apprehended, and he had been sentenced to life in prison at Waupun, where he still is to this day, as far as I know. That would have been April 1943."

He Doesn't Miss Much

Lee Remmel graduated from Shawano (Wisconsin) High School in 1944. He worked for the *Shawano County Journal* from 1940 to 1941 and for the *Green Bay Press-Gazette* from 1941 to 1974. He has worked for the Green Bay Packers since 1974 and is one of few men who have attended every Super Bowl game.

Daley: "Of course in those days we did all our writing on typewriters."

Remmel: "The one thing I liked about the typewriter, in retrospect, is that your story didn't vanish on you, as it occasionally does with computers. That's happened to me several times, to my great embarrassment and chagrin."

Daley: "I still write a column, and I use a typewriter."

Remmel: "I use a computer. I think I've adapted to it fairly well, but I still get frustrated when something vanishes, and that happens, sometimes inexplicably."

Daley: "I write for *Packer Report*. And I make a carbon. I don't know why. I put the carbon in a drawer, and after the season is over I throw them away."

Remmel: "You're the Lone Ranger there."

Daley: "I get so damned mad, trying to buy a typewriter ribbon. You can't find them anywhere."

Remmel: "Does that tell you something?"

Daley: "I turn in my stories on paper, and they input them. I've told them, 'I'm not going to get into that computer.' "

Remmel: "It was harder to write on deadline with typewriters than it is with computers. Of course there weren't any Thursday night or Sunday night or Monday night games back then. They were mostly Sunday afternoon games. The paper didn't come out until the next day, and you had all night to work on your story. I traveled with the team some of the time back then. Art traveled all the time. I went to Minnesota, Detroit. . . . Starting in 1967, I went to all the games on the road."

Daley: "We traveled by train. That's all there was in the '40s and '50s. I remember the first time I went to California was near the end of the '48 season. We played the Giants in Milwaukee and got clobbered [49–3], then we flew from Milwaukee to the West Coast in a Constellation to play the Los Angeles Rams. I think that was the first time I flew commercial. It was rough as hell going over the mountains, up and down. In the bus after, on the way to the Ojai Valley Inn, a lot of players were sick, throwing up. They stopped the bus a couple times. Nolan Luhn [an end who played for Green Bay] had to get out and puke."

Remmel: "My first flight was in '57, on a C–47 to Pittsburgh. It was a real white-knuckler."

Daley: "I never flew to the West Coast again until the mid-'50s. I remember going in to see my boss—I think it must have been 1952, when the Packers had a 6–6 season—and saying, 'We ought to cover those games out there.' And he agreed. A. B. Turnbull was there at the time [as the *Press-Gazette's* business manager]. He was a factor, too."

Remmel: "A. B. Turnbull deserves a lot of credit for the survival of the Packers. He's the one who turned the team into a business. Before that, they were flying by the seat of their pants. As I understand it, there was a torrential rainstorm on the morning of a game against Minneapolis in 1922. Turnbull and some of the top businessmen in town, who were like a committee of sorts, were discussing what to do. Do they play the game, or not? Turnbull finally said, 'Let's play the game and set ourselves apart from the colleges. We'll play in any kind of weather.' Some people credit him with establishing the NFL policy of playing in just about any kind of weather."

Daley: "I remember going to league meetings when Bert Bell was the commissioner, and we'd play poker. All those guys played poker, and Bell would walk around the back of the table and kibbutz. That's the way he was."

Remmel: "It was a family affair. It's not that way anymore, that's for sure. It's a multibillion-dollar business. The games are Sunday events, but they always have been Sunday events in Green Bay. I remember when women would dress to the nines. They'd wear their furs."

Daley: "And the men wore a hat, shirt, and a tie."

Remmel: "Of course we didn't play a lot of late-December games then. The season was over. They weren't wearing snow-mobile suits because they didn't need them."

Daley: "You didn't have warm clothing then. Even in the championship game out here in 1961, you look at some of those pictures, they've got those hats with the flaps pulled over their ears and those mackinaws. Nobody had down parkas or this thermal insulated stuff."

On Bart Starr's ill-fated tenure as coach of the Packers and the team's decline in the 1970s and 1980s

Daley: "When you look back, Lee, I think Dan Devine [the preceding coach] really hurt Starr badly with the John Hadl trade."

Remmel: "That certainly handicapped him. Bart was hamstrung for two or three years there. The Packers gave up two first-round draft choices, two second-rounders, and a third-rounder for Hadl. That's a lot to give up. The ironic part was Hadl was pretty well washed up when we got him. In retrospect, what really astounds me about having made the trade—

Coach Vince Lombardi (left) and Art Daley examine the pages of the first Green Bay Packers yearbook in 1960. According to Daley, Lombardi was concerned that the yearbook would somehow have a negative impact on ticket sales. Lombardi's worries were soon put to rest, and Lambeau Field has been sold out for every home game since. (Courtesy Art Daley)

except I knew Devine always coveted the guy; he even tried to recruit him at the University of Missouri—was that we had played the Rams in Milwaukee a few weeks prior to the trade. Hadl was mediocre, at best. The Packers won, 17–6, with young Jerry Tagge at quarterback. I think Hadl completed two passes all day. That ought to tell you something, but apparently that didn't get through to old D. D."

Daley: "This has been my own theory. If Bart would have taken after his father, who was an Air Force master sergeant. . . . "

Remmel: "He was a tough hombre."

Daley: ". . . he'd be on the sidelines chewing tobacco and spitting and cussing like a trooper. But Bart took after his mother. He was a real Southern gentleman."

Remmel: "I'll tell you, though, there was a lot of steel in Bart. He was a gentleman, but there was a lot of steel in him, as a player and as a competitor."

Daley: "He fired [assistant coach] Dave Hanner. I couldn't understand that, because of the kind of guy Bart was."

Remmel: "I think he leaned a little too heavily on his friends. He let Bill Curry [Starr's offensive line coach] and people like that make personnel decisions. That's what I think. And obviously, we made some wretched decisions."

Daley: "Those drafts were terrible. He could have had Joe Montana."

Remmel: "I remember, for example—not that they followed each other—but Mike Holmgren, when he first came here, he sat me down one day and said, 'Lee, what do you think has been the problem here?' I said, 'Well, I'm certainly not a football expert by any means, but I think a huge problem has been that we've done a miserable job of drafting in the first round.' Rich Campbell, Alphonso Carreker—he was a great traffic

Art Daley (left), Vernon Biever (center), and Lee Remmel have more than 150 years of collective experience watching and chronicling the Green Bay Packers. All three have been inducted into the Green Bay Packer Hall of Fame as contributors—in 1993, 2002, and 1996, respectively. (Courtesy Art Daley)

director, but that's about all. When you look back at that whole decade of the '80s, Sterling Sharpe was probably the only outstanding player who was drafted in the first round."

Daley: "Isn't that the truth?"

Remmel: "I just kind of accepted it. We were still in the league and we were still filling the stadium. Had the attendance started to decline dramatically, I would have been concerned. But that never happened. Maybe that's what lulled some other people into a false sense of security. Hey, the bottom line is good. Not to worry."

On Don Hutson, a Hall of Fame receiver–defensive back considered to be among the greatest football players of all time

Remmel: "I think Don Hutson was an artist. He was phenomenal. I saw him catch four touchdown passes and score twenty-nine points in one quarter. It was 1945, the last year he played. The exact date was October 7, 1945, at State Fair Park in Milwaukee, against the Detroit Lions. I was a cityside reporter, and I had gone to the sports editor—Art was in the service— and said, 'If I pay my expenses to Milwaukee, would you let me cover the game?' I wanted to show him I could write sports. He said, 'Go ahead.' The score was nothing to nothing at the end of the first quarter, it was 7–0 early in the second quarter, and by halftime, the Packers led, 41–7. They scored forty-one unanswered points. That's still the most points scored in one quarter of an NFL game; it's been tied but never broken. Hutson caught four touchdown passes in that quarter and kicked five extra points and scored twenty-nine points. As far as I've been able to determine, that's the most points ever scored by one player in one quarter of an NFL game. The Packers won, 57–21, and the fifty-seven points to this day is the most points they have ever scored in a league game. I interviewed the Lions coach, Gus Dorais, after the game—by the way, he was on the throwing end of the first forward pass ever thrown in college football, to Knute Rockne—and I said, 'Gus, would you sum it up for me?' He said, 'I'll give it to you in three words: Too much Hutson.' Talk about lucking out. That's a great memory for me. By the way, Hutson retired as the leading scorer and the leading receiver in professional football, and he also was the number-two interceptor in professional football. And he also kicked short-range field goals and extra points. Not a bad football player."

Daley: "He had flat feet, too."

Remmel: "But he ran a 9.7 100 yard dash, so they couldn't have been too flat. He could run. He was quite a baseball player, too. He batted .375 for the University of Alabama varsity his senior year."

Daley: "Hutson would have been a hell of a player in any era, even today. But back then, all the fastest players were on offense. The defensive players were not like they are today, where the fastest players are cornerbacks."

Remmel: "I asked Curly in 1965, 'How do you think Hutson would fare today?' He said, 'I think he would be more successful today than he was when he played.' Here was his rationale: He said, 'We'd only use him on offense. He'd never play defense.' Because he played both ways. Curly said, 'We never split him out back then, and we'd split him out now, flank him out wide and let him go one on one with a cornerback.' Don had great speed and big hands. He had huge hands. He was truly a great athlete."

On legendary coach Vince Lombardi

Remmel: "I'd say Lombardi was intimidating. Yeah, definitely. Particularly after he started winning."

Daley: "Inititally, I don't think he was bad."

Remmel: "The more success he had, the more arrogant he got."

Daley: "He was the kind of guy, he could hug you or kiss you. He could kiss you or punch you out. I always said he was chewing nails. He was never really happy, you know? And you wonder about his cancer, how the stress affected him."

Remmel: "Even though Lombardi had a totally different personality than Lambeau, he was likewise extremely confident. I remember at his first press conference, he said, 'You will be proud of the Packers, because I will be proud of the Packers.' I thought, 'Who the hell is this guy?' I had never heard word one about him. It's amazing, when I think about it. A year or two later, everybody knew who he was. He was a presence, no doubt about that."

On their favorite players through the years

Daley: "I liked Henry Jordan, because you always got a story out of him."

Remmel: "I personally was fond of Jerry Kramer and still am, in part because he was a very engaging guy, but also professionally because he was a great interview. If I were in desperate need of a story, all I had to do was get out my pad and pencil and ask him a question, and he'd write my column for me, almost literally. He had a great sense of what you were looking for. There aren't many guys like that. He was amazingly good and still is."

Daley: "Of course you've got to mention Paul Hornung. I think Hornung was like Lombardi would have liked to have been. I'll say this about Hornung: He never argued about money. He signed his contract right away."

Remmel: "I tell you what, he doesn't sign his autographs for free now. He's very fussy about that."

Daley: "All those guys make money now. Even Tony Canadeo. He gets a kick out of that. He always says, 'Who would want my autograph?'" *[Canadeo passed away eight months after this interview, at the age of 84.]*

Remmel: "Tony was our first 1,000-yard rusher. I know he was the third back in NFL history to rush for 1,000 yards. Beattie Feathers, Steve Van Buren, then Tony."

Daley: "He's the last of his kind."

Remmel: "He took a lot of knocks. He was a tough hombre. He had to be. They didn't have face masks on their helmets when he played. I don't know if he's got all his teeth or not, but he played hard."

You Could Look It Up

According to the Packers' media guide, during the 1923 season the team signed a player named Jack "Dollie" Gray, an end who had received All-America honors at Princeton.

At least, that's what Packers Coach Curly Lambeau was led to believe.

Gray started for Green Bay in a 24–3 loss to the Racine Legion. He played so poorly that Lambeau became suspicious and checked into the player's background, only to discover that Gray was an imposter. Lambeau booted him off the team.

Because Gray did play in a game, however, the Packers still list him on their all-time roster.

On quarterback Brett Favre

Daley: "He's a hell of a guy."

Remmel: "Not only is he a great player, but the sheer joy he plays with is contagious. I think he's a phenomenal athlete."

Daley: "You wonder how he's going to end it all."

Remmel: "Everybody has developed their own conclusions about what he's said. I wouldn't pretend to know what he's thinking, but it certainly does sound like he's not going to play a lot longer. I think his mortality has begun to concern him a little bit."

Daley: "One thing about him, he keeps a low profile."

Art Daley (left) shares a private moment with National Football League Commissioner Paul Tagliabue before Super Bowl XXVI in Minneapolis in 1991. (Courtesy Art Daley)

Remmel: "I tell you what, he's become a very good family man. He's got a lovely wife. She's a great gal. His kids are really nice, too."

Daley: "I see him all the time at Oneida [Golf & Riding Club], on the driving range. I say, 'Brett, do you want me to get over here or over there? You don't want to look at me.' Last year, I'm out at practice one day, and he comes off the field and I say, 'Damn, you're only thirty-two years old.' He says, 'How old are you, Art?'"

Remmel: "He's a very natural, down-home guy. But he's a very shrewd guy, too. Don't let him kid you about that. Mike Sherman said, 'He could be anything he wanted to be. If he wanted to be a surgeon, he could be one. He's got that kind of intelligence.' I tell you what, he does a great job with the media. He never, ever says anything foolish, which doesn't surprise me because he's the son of a coach."

Daley: "He's a hell of a golfer, too. He's down to a two handicap out at Oneida. He shot a 69 one day. I told him one day that he should play in that thing that the tour has with the NFL. He said he didn't have time."

Remmel: "He's probably too busy riding his tractor."

Daley: "He keeps a low profile, for who he is."

On their longevity, and the resilience of the Packers organization

Daley: "I guess the thing is to stay active. I still do a lot of writing and reading. I've been lucky enough to keep close to the Packers. They still furnish me a seat in the press box. I still write a column. Lee and I are the last two guys connected with Curly Lambeau, in our capacity, anyway."

Remmel: "I've missed one game since 1967. The only game I missed was when my father died."

Daley: "I think we've been lucky from the standpoint that our health has been good. I've been fortunate as hell. I'm eighty-six."

Remmel: "That's exactly the point I make. I've seen more than one hundred consecutive Packers–Bears games. If I hadn't been healthy . . . all I have to have is a virus one weekend and it's over. I've seen every game the Packers and Bears have played since 1946. I've seen every game in the Packers–Viking series."

Daley: "One of the things I still like about writing a column is there are a lot of things you can dig up. I'll tell you one thing:

Having contributed to more than three dozen Green Bay Packers year-books and covered the team for much of his life, Art Daley is among the most knowledgeable men in the world on the subject of all things green and gold. (Courtesy Art Daley)

Our decade of the 1950s was the worst in the league until the Cincinnati Bengals broke it last year. From 1948 through '58, we were losers."

Remmel: "I remember it well."

Daley: "When you think about it, it's amazing they built the stadium [in 1957]."

Remmel: "A remarkable display of optimism. It really was. They built a stadium for a team that was 4–9 every year."

Daley: "I tell you, Bert Bell always said what makes this game great is the shape of the ball. You never know what's going to happen."

Remmel: "I think the Packers are an incredible story. I never tire talking of it."

Daley: "We live it every day—you, especially, Lee. You can't get away from it. Just look at that stadium across the street."

Remmel: "I sound like a house man, but I think we owe a great debt of gratitude to Bob Harlan for pushing the renovation project. First of all, conceiving it, and then leading the charge to get it done. Because that was the only way we could guarantee the team surviving for the long term. No question about that. A lot of people were very short-sighted. They couldn't picture what he was telling them, which was the exact truth: 'If we don't do this, we won't be around long.' "

On things they don't like about the modern NFL

Daley: "You know what I don't like now? This fumble stuff. They say the ground can't cause a fumble. That's like giving the offense an extra player. It's a crutch. That's a load of crap. If you lose the ball, no matter how you lose it, it should be a fumble. Hang on to the ball."

Remmel: "What irks me is the conduct. I hate these guys who do the dances and that kind of stuff. I personally commend

Emmitt Smith, who just hands the ball to the official. Barry Sanders and Walter Payton did the same thing. Some people say, 'I kind of like the dancing.' To each his own, but I don't like it."

Daley: "Especially when they're losing the game."

Remmel: "That's right. To me, that's too individual. Football allegedly is a team game. You see guys doing dances after they get a sack and their team is losing, 28–0. That's a bad joke."

Chester Marcol:
Alive and Kicking

Among the lessons Dan Devine learned during his first season as head coach of the Packers in 1971 was that having a dependable placekicker was more important to a team's success in the National Football League than it was in the college ranks.

Devine learned this lesson the hard way, because the Packers did not have a dependable placekicker in 1971. Despite the instant impact of rookie running back John Brockington, who rushed for 1,105 yards, the Packers could manage only a 4–8–2 record. Had they scored just three more points—one field goal—in every game, their record would have been 9–5.

Erratic kicking was not a new problem in Green Bay. The franchise had gone through nine kickers between 1968 and 1971: Mike Mercer, Jerry Kramer, Chuck Mercein, Erroll Mann, Booth Lustig, Dale Livingston, Lou Michaels, Tim Webster, and Dave Conway. They had combined to make just thirty-three field goals in seventy-four attempts, a pitiful 44.5 percent success rate.

Devine suffered through Michaels, Webster, and Conway in 1971, and after watching them go a combined fourteen for twenty-six, the coach decided he had seen enough. He vowed to take a kicker in the early rounds of the 1972 NFL draft, and he was intrigued by a Polish immigrant from tiny Hillsdale College, in Michigan, named Chester Marcol.

Marcol was born Czeslaw Boleslaw Marcol on October 24, 1949. He grew up in Opole, Poland, the son of a member of the Communist Party. "We were forbidden to go to church," Marcol said. "But yet, every year, I spent a month at my cousin's house with an uncle who wasn't a member [of the Communist Party], so we went to church. I remember those big cathedral churches."

Life wasn't easy in post–World War II Poland, but Marcol had a happy childhood. A natural athlete, he excelled at soccer and was the goalie on his country's national junior team.

But his life took a sudden and wrenching turn in March 1964. One day that month, his father came home from work, went into his bedroom, put a gun to his head, and pulled the trigger. With no way to provide for her four children, the widowed Anna Marcol had no choice but live with her parents—and they had emigrated to the United States and worked on vegetable farms near Imlay City, Michigan. "My grandparents and uncles and aunts were vegetable farmers, hard-working people," Marcol said. "They all lived in one house with no bathrooms. My two aunts, their husbands, my uncle, and my grandma and grandpa. Men were getting paid twenty-five cents an hour to work on the farm. Women were getting paid a dime an hour."

Young Czeslaw, just fifteen, spoke no English and was miserable those first few months in America. "I hated it here at first," he said. "Imlay City was such a change because I was used to Opole. I was a teenager, my father had just died, I didn't speak any English. I hated it."

Marcol was enrolled at Imlay City High School. A cousin was in the same grade and acted as an interpreter. Marcol took basic Spanish classes with English-speaking students so he could learn how to speak English. Reading just a few pages of a homework assignment was an exercise in frustration, because he had to look up nearly every word in a Polish–English dictionary. Many nights, the painstaking effort drove him to tears.

Then, one rainy day, his physical education class played soccer in the gymnasium. Soccer was one language "Chester"— his Americanized name—knew well. He was selected to take a penalty kick. The teacher, John Rowan, was the goalie. Marcol placed the ball down 10 yards from Rowan and took out all his pain and frustration in that kick. The ball whistled past Rowan's ear so quickly he barely managed to turn his head. It smacked off the wall behind him and rebounded into his face, bloodying his nose.

The next day, Rowan, who also was a football coach at the high school, took Chester out to a field and emptied a sack of oddly shaped balls. Marcol thought they were rugby balls. Rowan placed one on a tee and pointed to the goal posts. Marcol understood. He kicked a 30-yard field goal, soccer style. Rowan moved the tee back to 35 yards, then to 40, then to 45. Marcol kept kicking the ball between the uprights.

Rowan and other men who were watching began talking excitedly.

"Czeslaw," Marcol's cousin told him, "they want you to play football."

"Football?" he said, only vaguely aware of the game. "Are they crazy?"

It didn't take long, however, for the idea to begin to appeal to Marcol. He loved sports and was a good athlete despite his diminutive stature (5'8" 150 pounds). He missed the action and excitement of soccer, and while football was a different game entirely, it was better than nothing at all.

"He was a natural," said Arlan Winslow, then one of Marcol's best friends and now the chief of police in Imlay City. "He had good hands. He was fast. He had good eye–hand coordination. He ran a lot of track and field, and he still holds a couple of high school records here. He was a hell of a baseball player, too."

Future Kicker Saw the Sneak

Although Marcol grew up in Imlay City, Michigan, he was a Packers fan and was in the Lambeau Field stands when Bart Starr—later his coach—scored the winning touchdown in the 1967 Ice Bowl game against the Dallas Cowboys. "I was sitting in the opposite end zone when Starr scored," Marcol said. "Half the stadium went crazy, and it took maybe a second before the other half even knew what happened."

Marcol played wide receiver, returned kicks and punts, and was Imlay City's punter and placekicker. In his first varsity game, he kicked three field goals to account for all of Imlay City's points in a 9–7 victory.

Most of his teammates happily accepted this Polish whiz, but a few players teased him about his broken English and thick accent. "I'll tell you a little story," Winslow said. "One of our big linemen used to harass him all the time. He was just having fun, but Chester got tired of it. He told me, 'You watch, I'll take care of him.' At practice one day, they're working on extra points. Chester kicks the ball, hits this guy square in the butt, and knocks him to the ground. Chester says, 'Missed that one, coach.' Then he says to me, 'I'm not done yet.' He knocked him down three times.

"He could put the ball wherever he wanted it. He could hit the square behind the basket [on a basketball backboard]. He could hit you on the dead run."

Marcol's grandfather didn't understand Czeslaw's fascination with these silly American games. His grandfather came from the old country and believed a strong young boy should come home after school and help with chores around the farm, so he refused to allow family members to pick up Marcol after practices. If Chester couldn't find a ride home, he had to walk several miles, sometimes in cold rain or through heavy snow.

But in the summers, there was no escaping the farm work. Marcol picked squash, cucumbers, and lettuce, crawling through the muck under the blazing sun. He wore flannel shirts to protect his arms from scratches. "I worked eighty hours a week," he said. "It was hard work, but I had no choice because the first or second Saturday in August, there was a sidewalk sale in town. I saved my money all summer and that's where we bought our school clothes. Two pair of shoes for ten bucks, nice winter jackets for twenty-four. By then I was making a buck an hour, so I was making $80 a week.

"We had tough times, but my mom never went to get a food stamp. We never got government help. We just ate what was on the farm. I remember many times for dinner eating spinach, eggs, and potatoes. But that was OK, you know? It was a meal."

With help from his high school coaches, Marcol earned an athletic scholarship to Hillsdale College in Michigan, where he went on to become an NAIA All-American kicker. He booted a 62-yard field goal against Fairmont College in 1969, one year before Tom Dempsey of the New Orleans Saints made his famous 63-yard game-winning kick against the Detroit Lions.

Once, in the closing seconds of a blowout victory over St. Norbert College, the Hillsdale coaches called a timeout and sent in Marcol to attempt a 77-yard field goal. "The referee told me if I had tried it from 73 or 75, it would have been good," Marcol said. "The ball went just under the crossbar."

In another game against St. Norbert on a rainy, windy day, Marcol twice attempted field goals from 69 yards. Both were long enough, but the wind blew them just outside the right upright. He routinely kicked 70-yarders in practice.

Marcol's powerful right leg was exactly what the Green Bay Packers needed in 1972. After taking cornerback Willie Buchanon and quarterback Jerry Tagge with his two first-round picks in the NFL draft, Devine tabbed Marcol in the second round. It wasn't long before the Packers realized he was something special. In the season opener Marcol kicked four field goals in a 26–10 victory over the Cleveland Browns. He kept kicking field goals that year until he had made thirty-three in forty-eight attempts, team records that still stand (although Ryan Longwell tied the former in 2000).

Marcol wore glasses and sported a mop of tightly curled hair and an ever-present smile. Packers fans took to him immediately. But it was what Marcol did to the hated Chicago Bears that first year that forever endeared him to the Green Bay faithful and put him high on the list of the Windy City's most scorned athletes.

In the preseason Shrine Game at Milwaukee County Stadium, Marcol's field goal with thirteen seconds left gave the Packers a 10–7 victory. On October 8, a blustery day at

Chester Marcol (13), a soccer-style kicker from Hillsdale College by way of tiny Imlay City, Michigan, had an enormous impact on the Packers as a rookie in 1972. He kicked 33 field goals and scored 128 points, helping Green Bay reach the playoffs. (Vernon J. Biever Photo)

Lambeau Field in Green Bay, he kicked two field goals in a 20–17 victory, including the game-winner from 37 yards with 30 seconds left.

After he made the latter, he had to kick off into a wind he estimated at 35 mph. "I was putting the ball on the tee and I said, 'Hell, with the wind this strong, they'll get the ball on the 40 yard line and they've got enough time to get into field goal range,' " Marcol said. "Their return man lined up on the 20 yard line. I was getting ready to kick, and I said, 'Chester, you've got a strong, strong leg. You will kick the ball so hard, you're going to knock it over that guy's head, and they're not going to return anything.'

"Well, I kicked it so hard the ball hit the crossbar. I've had a lot of great moments playing football, but that was one of my personal proudest moments. If I'd had the wind behind me on that one, it probably would have gone into the seats. Probably very few people, if any, would remember that play. But that is a very proud moment for me."

Bears fans are more likely to remember what Marcol did to their team in their third and final meeting of 1972. On November 12, at Soldier Field in Chicago, he kicked three more field goals, the last of which came with 1:46 remaining and iced a 23–17 victory.

You have to understand the long and bitter rivalry that exists between the Packers and the Bears to grasp exactly what this meant to both franchises. Bears Coach Abe Gibron

A Dynamic Debut

As a rookie in 1972, Chester Marcol not only broke the Packers team record for field goals made in a season, he shattered it. Marcol kicked thirty-three field goals that year, fourteen more than the previous franchise record held by Don Chandler and one less than the National Football League record at the time. Marcol's 128 total points that season fell one short of the NFL record for scoring by an exclusive kicker.

couldn't stomach losing to the Packers in general, and especially when the right foot of a foreign-born, soccer-style kicker was inflicting all the damage. So Gibron devised a strategy for revenge. He designated special teams player Gary Kosins to go after Marcol on kickoffs with specific instructions: Knock his block off. If Kosins couldn't get in a good lick, he would at least try to put the fear of God into Marcol, and maybe give him something to think about besides kicking game-winning field goals. When the Packers loudly objected to the tactic, Gibron snorted, "Who do they think he is, a Polish prince?"

Ironically, Kosins also was Polish—his parents had dropped the "ki" from Kosinski—and his family was from Milwaukee. "All I know was that when we played Green Bay that was the big thing: Intimidate Chester Marcol," Kosins said. "Most kickers will at least make a halfhearted attempt to draw you off or sidestep you and stay on the field. Chester Marcol would run for the sidelines as fast as he could. Maybe he was smart. Maybe he was protecting his leg. I don't know."

Marcol remembered his confrontations with Kosins differently. "Yeah, there was a little pushing and shoving," he said. "I grabbed his face mask one time and gave it a twist. So many times, we just did some titty bumping."

Marcol led the NFL in scoring that year with 128 points and was named rookie of the year and All-Pro. But it wasn't just his field goals that made him so valuable to the Packers. He kicked off seventy-five times and recorded twenty-nine touchbacks. On the other 46 kickoffs, the average return was only 20.2 yards, which meant opposing teams rarely started a drive from beyond their own 20 yard line. The average return for all seventy-five kickoffs was only 12.4 yards. Time and again, he pinned opponents deep in their own territory, and the Packers consistently won the crucial battle of field position.

Not coincidentally, Green Bay finished with a 10–4 record and won the National Football Conference Central Division title. The Packers would not appear in the playoffs again, outside of the strike-shortened 1982 season, for more than twenty years.

Arguably, no rookie has ever made a bigger impact on the Packers than did Marcol in 1972. Chester Marcol fan clubs sprouted up throughout Wisconsin, and he was embraced by the large Polish community in Milwaukee. During games at County Stadium, it wasn't unusual to see the flag of Poland on proud display in the stands. It was heady stuff for a twenty-three-year-old immigrant who had kicked a football for the first time just seven years earlier.

Marcol again led the NFL in scoring with ninety-four points in 1974 and was named All-Pro. In his first three years in the league, he made a combined 79 of 122 field goal attempts and scored 304 points, or 42.4 percent of the Packers' 716 points.

However, injuries and personal problems would haunt Marcol for the rest of his career. He played eight-plus years for the Packers, but after his third season, he never again kicked more than thirteen field goals or scored more than fifty-four points in a season.

He did, however, enjoy one final moment of glory late in his career. That it occurred in a game against the Chicago Bears made it all the more satisfying.

The Packers went into the 1980 season opener against the Bears in disarray. They had had only two winning seasons in the 1970s and were coming off a 5–11 record, having lost seven of their last nine games in 1979. Furthermore, they had failed to win a game in the preseason and had been outscored,

86–17, by five opponents. Four days before the regular-season opener at Lambeau Field, Fred Von Appen, the team's line coach, resigned.

That was the backdrop to the game Packers fans fondly refer to as "Marcol's Miracle."

In a defensive struggle in which neither the Packers nor the Bears could find the end zone, Marcol kicked field goals of 41 and 46 yards but was matched by Chicago's Bob Thomas, who booted two of 41 and 34 yards. The game went into overtime tied, 6–6.

A 32-yard pass from Packers quarterback Lynn Dickey to wide receiver James Lofton set up Marcol's 34-yard attempt to win the game. But Bears defensive lineman Alan Page got a good push up the middle and leaped high just as Marcol's foot connected with the ball. It slammed into the face mask of Page's helmet and rebounded directly into Marcol's hands.

For a pregnant second nobody in the stadium knew what had happened. Then, there was Marcol, running left toward the end zone, with the ball cradled awkwardly in his arms. Only one Chicago player had even a remote chance to catch the galloping Polish Prince, and his path was impeded by the Packers' Jim Gueno, who seemed to be the only player on the field aware that Marcol had the ball.

Marcol scored the touchdown and was mobbed by his teammates. The Packers had won, 12–6.

"I was a soccer goalie and I had real good hands," Marcol said. "That ball came to me so quick . . . instinct took over and I just booked. I didn't see anybody. I was running as fast as I could. I was so open I could have walked in backwards. The thing I can't forget is that all my teammates jumped on me, and I couldn't get out of the pile. People were beating on me.

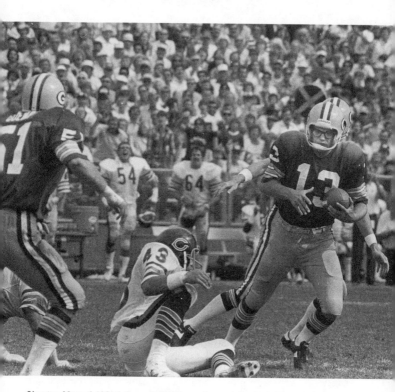

Chester Marcol (13) takes off for the end zone after catching his own blocked field goal against the Chicago Bears in the 1980 season opener. Marcol's improbable touchdown gave the Packers a 12–6 overtime victory and further enhanced his reputation as a "Bear killer." (Vernon J. Biever Photo)

"It was a moment that I will never forget. Every time I walk into Lambeau, I look at that corner of the end zone. It's been voted the fourth-most popular play in Packers history."

In the locker room after the game, Coach Bart Starr presented Marcol with the game ball. With tears of joy running down his cheeks, the kicker led the team in prayer.

As sweet as that moment was for Marcol, he was spiraling out of control off the field. Weeks earlier, he had discovered cocaine. He already had a problem with alcohol, and his new drug of choice was rapidly consuming him. "That was the straw that broke the camel's back," he said. "When I started using cocaine, everything just crashed. Just crashed. I thought I could use it recreationally, but I'm the kind of person that, after a while, I wanted lots of it."

Not surprisingly, his marriage was unraveling, too. Marcol had never shed a tear over his alcoholic father's suicide and didn't know how to talk about the anger and bitterness he had harbored all these years. During one argument at home, his wife, Barbara, screamed, "You're just like your father!" Marcol reacted by throwing a glass into the fireplace.

"I had everything bottled up," he said. "How in the world could I talk? My greatest thing was that defense. Anger. I would get angry at people."

Marcol's Baptist minister approached one of the Packers coaches and asked if the team was aware that Marcol had serious problems at home and was using drugs. "I don't think they had a clue," Marcol said. He knew he had a serious problem but was too afraid to ask for help. In 1980 the NFL dealt much differently with players who had substance abuse problems than it does today. "If a player needs help now, he gets it immediately," Marcol said. "Back then, they would boot you out of the league."

On October 8, just thirty-one days after Marcol scored his memorable game-winning touchdown against the Bears, Starr released him and signed kicker Tom Birney. The official reason was that the Packers were not satisfied with the length of Marcol's kickoffs, and it was true that his leg was not as strong as it once was. But the real reason Marcol was let go was that the Packers couldn't get a handle on his drug use.

After a brief stint with the Houston Oilers, Marcol was out of football. The most money he had ever made in one season was $100,000, but that was long gone. He was consuming huge quantities of cocaine and binge drinking. He tried to quit but couldn't. He went into rehabilitation but relapsed. And so the cycle continued: Over and over, he sobered up only to be drawn back in.

"You can't imagine the shame and guilt," he said. "But yet, an amazing thing happens. The shame and guilt and feeling so rotten on the inside, and feeling like I had just totally failed, is not enough to stop you. It's a disease. Some people still have a hard time comprehending that. A lot of them say, 'All it takes is willpower.' I tell them, 'The next time you have diarrhea, see how much willpower you have.'"

In 1986 Marcol hit rock bottom. He attempted suicide by drinking battery acid, an unfortunate event that left him with a severely damaged esophagus. But it was the turning point in his life, the episode that put him on the tenuous, day-to-day path of sobriety. "It's a sensitive subject," Marcol said. "Yes, I'm an alcoholic. That's a fact of life. That's part of me, and it's never been a secret. It's not always been the easiest thing, but I do my best. I hang around with a lot of people who don't drink. I go to my twelve-step program and that helps. And I go on."

Marcol went back to Hillsdale and got his degree in health science and physical education, then took a job as a residential counselor for troubled young men in Albion, Michigan. "That was more rewarding than anything I ever did, maybe even the NFL," he said. "Even my sponsor, that's what he says: 'Maybe that's why God kept you alive, Chester. You can witness to people who have problems. You can share your experience, strength, and hope. And there isn't anybody who has a story like yours.' "

In the early 1990s Marcol moved to Dollar Bay, a small town near the top of Michigan's Upper Peninsula, about a four-and-one-half-hour drive north of Green Bay. He has worked odd jobs, including doing radio commentary for the Michigan Tech University football team. He remarried, and he and his wife, Carole, have three children. But he has not spoken to Julie, his daughter from his first marriage, for many years. "Maybe she will contact me, but I can only make so many amends," Marcol said. "I'm not going to sit and write every week, 'I'm sorry for this, I'm sorry for that.' I made my amends. If she wants to come around, she'll come around."

Marcol's health is not good. He contracted hepatitis C from a blood transfusion in the 1980s and must have annual liver biopsies. He was on medication for a while but stopped taking it because he didn't like the side effects. He has had surgery on his elbow three times. Three or four times a year, he must undergo an unpleasant outpatient procedure in which he is sedated and progressively larger tubes are inserted down his throat to stretch his damaged esophagus.

"At one time, they thought they would have to remove my esophagus," Marcol said. "They were going to make a new esophagus for me, either from the intestine or the colon. [But,] it's getting much better."

In 2002 he was diagnosed with a heart condition called ventricular tachycardia. Doctors implanted a defibrillator in his chest, which shocks his heart into a normal rhythm when it starts beating too fast. The defibrillator has recorded dozens of "silent episodes" that he didn't feel and one big one, a shock that knocked him to his knees and scared him.

Marcol quit smoking cigarettes cold turkey and said he has not touched cocaine for years. "Can you imagine, with my heart, if I took any kind of drug that stimulated me?" he said. "I'd probably be dead in an hour. This [defibrillator] is set to go off at 162 [heartbeats per minute]. Can you imagine shooting up? This thing would probably end up in the next block."

All of the medical procedures, tests, and operations cost money, and Marcol has little of that to spare. He is on Social Security disability and receives a noninjury football disability pension from the NFL. Occasionally, he makes a little money at autograph-signing shows but otherwise has no other source of income.

"If I didn't have any medical bills, we would do okay," he said. "It's kind of hard to shell out $300 or $400 a month when you're on a fixed income. I make payments to so many hospitals, so many doctors. But I have to have things done. What are you going to do?

"But you know what? People have been kind. Everybody has been kind. I make my payments, whatever I can afford. Sometimes more, sometimes less."

Marcol was inducted into the Green Bay Packers Hall of Fame in 1987. The late Domenic Gentile, the team's long-time trainer, presented him. Gentile said he thought Marcol could have kicked in the NFL for a decade longer had he not gotten involved with drugs. We'll never know, but in the mid-1990s, when Marcol worked as a volunteer coach with the Houghton (Michigan) High School football team, he easily kicked 45-yard field goals in tennis shoes.

"I believe today that everything happens the way it's supposed to happen," Marcol said. "But, unfortunately, I induced several of these things. I believe I cheated myself, whatever you want to say, because I made those choices."

At the conclusion of the 2002 season, Marcol still ranked sixth on the Packers all-time scoring list with 521 points. He is proud of his game-winning field goals and his Pro Bowl appearances. But he is proudest of the fact that no opponent ever returned one of his kickoffs for a touchdown, on any level—high school, college, or the NFL.

"The guy that hurt me the most was Walter Payton [the late Bears running back]," Marcol said. "He returned kicks early in his career. One time, he broke free, and I was the last guy between him and the end zone. I had an angle on him, and he stiff-armed me and knocked me off him like I was a dead duck. But I was able to slow him down enough so that somebody else tackled him. My neck was stiff for three days after that. Jim Carter, our middle linebacker, said, 'See how strong he is? We get that all the time.'

"In college, against Ashland, this guy broke through and was headed for the end zone. I was pretty fast then and I had an angle and I went with all my might. I grabbed him by the belt and jerked him down at about the 5 yard line. That was the closest anybody ever got to returning one of my kicks for a touchdown."

Marcol remains a hugely popular figure among Packers fans. During player introductions at the annual Alumni Game at Lambeau Field, he always receives one of the loudest ovations. He also claims to be one of the team's biggest fans and never misses a game on television.

"I get shaky before games," he said. "A lot of times, I feel just like I'm walking in the tunnel before the game starts. I get out of control. I'm almost sick to my stomach. I love the Packers."

Tony Mandarich's Comeback

This is a story about personal and professional redemption. It is the story of Ante Josip "Tony" Mandarich, who went from being an enormously gifted and cocksure number two pick in the 1989 college draft to the dubious distinction of being one of the biggest busts in National Football League history.

In NFL scout-speak, Mandarich, a 300-pound mountain of fast-twitch muscle fiber, "looked like Tarzan, played like Jane." He was not the first flop, nor would he be the last, but few flameouts were more spectacular than that of this one-time *Sports Illustrated* cover boy.

Mandarich left the game a broken and bitter man, humiliated by his experience with the Green Bay Packers and haunted by his unfulfilled promise.

That could have been the end of the story.

But there was more to Mandarich than met the eye, and what met the eye was considerable. After sitting out three years, he made a remarkable comeback, one that many never would have thought possible. He signed with the Indianapolis Colts as a minimum-salary free agent, made the team as a long shot, eventually moved into the starting lineup, and played well until a shoulder injury forced his retirement.

There are lessons to be learned from the "Tony Mandarich Story." Lessons about personal growth and perseverance. Lessons about pride and dignity.

And so, it is a story worth retelling.

Mandarich is a Canadian native, born and raised in Oakville, Ontario. He attended White Oaks High School for three years and then moved to Ohio to live with his older brother, John, who was playing football at Kent State University. Mandarich enrolled at Kent Roosevelt High School, where he won All-Metro honors as a guard on the football team. Over his high school career, he won four letters in football, three in wrestling, and one each in baseball and basketball.

But it was in East Lansing, Michigan, where Mandarich made a name for himself.

He was a three-year starter at left tackle at Michigan State University, where the head coach, George Perles, called him "the finest offensive lineman I have ever been associated with." During his senior year in 1988, the 6'5" Mandarich was a man among boys, plowing down anything that got in his way and opening gaping holes for the Spartans' powerful running game, which averaged 246 yards per game.

For an offensive lineman, there is nothing more satisfying than knocking an opposing player off his feet. Mandarich recorded at least ten such "pancake" blocks in every game but one, including a season-high seventeen against Purdue. He was amazingly quick and agile for a 300-pound man and played hard and mean from snap to whistle. Plus, his strength was off the charts, thanks to a weight-lifting regimen that bordered on the obsessive.

Mandarich helped the Spartans reach the Rose Bowl as a senior and was a unanimous first-team All-American. He was named the College Lineman of the Year by both the Washington, D.C., and Columbus, Ohio, Touchdown Clubs.

The only question was how high he would go in the 1989 NFL draft.

The league's scouts and general managers had watched him develop into a one-man wrecking crew at Michigan State. At the National Scouting Combine and in individual workouts, he tested so well that he was labeled a "blue chip" prospect, an impact player who would immediately move into the starting lineup of any team that picked him and probably would become a Pro Bowl–caliber performer within two or three years.

Mandarich had no discernible weaknesses. He could squat lift 550 pounds and run the 40-yard dash in an almost superhuman time of 4.65 seconds while weighing 303 pounds. He recorded a standing broad jump of 10 feet, 3 inches and a vertical leap of thirty inches. In the twenty-one years the Scouting Combine had rated draft-eligible college players, only Herschel Walker and Bo Jackson graded higher.

The NFL's general managers had only two concerns about Mandarich. One was the lingering suspicion that he had come by his strength pharmaceutically. The other was his inexperience as a pass blocker in Michigan State's run-oriented offense. But he never tested positive for steroids—during or after college—and most NFL scouts thought he would adjust easily to the pro passing game because of his quick feet and athletic ability.

After the Dallas Cowboys selected quarterback Troy Aikman with the first pick of the 1989 draft, the Packers grabbed Mandarich. They could have taken running back

Barry Sanders, linebacker Derrick Thomas, or cornerback Deion Sanders—all of whom would go on to have careers worthy of Hall of Fame consideration—but they figured Mandarich would anchor their offensive line for a decade.

No offensive lineman or Canadian had ever been drafted so high by an NFL team.

Sports Illustrated did a cover story on a bare-chested Mandarich, headlined "The Incredible Bulk." People compared him with Anthony Munoz, considered one of the best offensive tackles in the history of the game.

Unfortunately, Mandarich started to believe all the hype.

He spurned the Packers' initial contract offer, hit the late-night talk show circuit, and hinted at a big-money prize fight with Mike Tyson. He lived in Los Angeles and pumped iron on Venice Beach. His only real passion seemed to be the music of heavy metal icons Guns N' Roses; he adorned himself with tattoos that glorified the band and named his dog after its lead singer, Axl Rose.

All the while, Mandarich should have been getting ready for training camp.

"I think in many ways, I set myself up [to fail]," Mandarich says now. "I wanted to create as much hype as I could for many different reasons: exposure, negotiation leverage, you name it. And it all worked.

"Except the performance wasn't there when it was time to play football."

Mandarich finally ended his holdout on September 5, 1989, signing a four-year contract worth $4.4 million. He had missed all of training camp and was not in football shape. In practice Packers defenders routinely blew by him in pass-blocking drills. He played stiff and didn't seem as strong or as quick as advertised.

Tony Mandarich never achieved the greatness predicted for him as the Packers' first-round draft choice in 1989. He walked away from the game after four disappointing seasons but made a remarkable comeback in the mid-1990s with the Indianapolis Colts. (Vernon J. Biever Photo)

If the Packers coaches were concerned, Mandarich was not. He bragged that he would be playing in the Pro Bowl before long. He dressed and acted the part of a rebel rocker, proudly displaying his many tattoos. He was immodest and obnoxious, and his act did not go over well with the team's blue-collar fans. He foolishly referred to Green Bay as a "village" and was quickly dubbed the "village idiot."

When he finally got on the field September 24, in a game against the Los Angeles Rams, he was shocked by his own ineffectiveness. "In college you can play against players that are average, and if you're a good player, you can look incredible," Mandarich says. "In the NFL, if you play against a team that has a 2–12 record and is playing out the string, well, the players are still good.

"That was absolutely an eye-opener."

He saw action in fourteen games as a rookie, solely as a reserve tackle and as a blocker on special teams. The next year, he started all sixteen regular-season games at right tackle and was adequate, though hardly the dominant force he was expected to be. He was solid as a run blocker but still struggled to protect the quarterback.

Mandarich continued to improve in 1991, starting the first fifteen games before a slight ligament tear in his left ankle forced him to sit out the final game of the season.

But the 1992 season was a washout. He reported to camp smaller and weaker than ever, which he attributed to a parasitic infection caused by drinking stream water on a bear hunt in Canada. Skeptics whispered that he had stopped taking steroids. Then, in an exhibition game on August 8 against Kansas City, he suffered a severe concussion. Later diagnosed with post-concussion syndrome and a thyroid condition, he sat out the entire 1992 season.

First-year Coach Mike Holmgren hadn't seen much of Mandarich, but he had seen enough. The Packers elected not to renew Mandarich's contract and released him on February 26, 1993.

Sports Illustrated did another story on Mandarich. This time, the headline read, "The Incredible Bust." The magazine quoted anonymous teammates who substantiated the widespread rumors of steroid abuse. To this day Mandarich claims he is innocent, but one thing is certain: No player drafted so high had ever promised so much and delivered so little.

Humiliated and bitter, Mandarich retreated to the log cabin he had built on his 160-acre property near Traverse City, Michigan, where he lived in virtual seclusion with his wife, Amber, and their daughter, Holly. He lost interest in football and vowed to never again play the game he once dominated.

His career totals in Green Bay: forty-five games played, thirty-one started.

"I didn't have the best experience playing in Green Bay, and the only person I can point my finger at is myself," Mandarich says. "At the time I pointed my finger at the media, the fans, the team. But it was all me."

While Mandarich was dealing with the disappointment and embarrassment of his miserable professional football career, he also underwent therapy to deal with the cancer-caused death of his brother. John Mandarich, a Canadian Football League veteran and Tony's mentor, was just thirty-one when he died in February 1993.

The Miami Dolphins and San Diego Chargers contacted Mandarich about a year into his retirement. He was obviously out of shape and his workouts went poorly. He was soft and slow and clearly lacked motivation.

Nobody wanted to sign him, and he didn't care.

Another year went by, and NFL fans forgot about Mandarich, except around draft time, when his name inevitably surfaced in discussions about the league's all-time biggest busts.

He attended Northwestern Michigan College in Traverse City and was working toward a degree in law enforcement. One morning, on his way to class, he stopped dead in his tracks. The leaves were turning colors, the air was crisp and cold, and he found himself thinking about football. Surprisingly, he realized he missed the game.

Mandarich weighed 265 pounds. He started thinking about a comeback. This time, he would do things the right way. "A lot of people in the business said, 'You won't do it. You've been out of the league too long. You've lost foot speed,'" Mandarich says. "I started working out, and I played a lot of racquetball to improve my foot speed.

"The thing was I didn't like the way it ended in Green Bay. Again, [it was] nothing that Green Bay or the Packers did wrong, but it left a bad taste in my mouth."

After six months in the weight room, Mandarich was back up to 326 pounds and was able to bench-press 225 pounds thirty-four times, ten above the average for offensive linemen at the 1996 National Scouting Combine. He ran the 40-yard dash in 5.0 seconds, not close to his speed seven years earlier but still better than average.

Gone was the brash and immature rock 'n' roll punk. In his place was a serious professional who just wanted a second chance.

The Indianapolis Colts needed help on their offensive line, and Coach Lindy Infante, who had drafted Mandarich in Green Bay, was intrigued by the player's rededication to football.

Still dogged by rumors of steroid use, Mandarich passed a drug test administered by the Colts. On February 22, 1996—nearly three years to the day after the Packers released him—he signed a two-year contract that paid him the league minimum of $196,000 the first year. "It's risk-free and I don't even like to call it a gamble," Infante said at the time. "I like to call it an experiment. The way I look at it is that we have very little risk at this attempt. He has dedicated himself to making one last attempt to play at this level. He's worked out very diligently for the last nine months or so. He's in good shape. He looks good, he worked out well, and he seems to be focused on what he's trying to prove."

Mandarich became a starter and played three years before a shoulder injury forced him to retire. There were no post-season trips to Hawaii for the Pro Bowl and few pancake blocks, but he was steady and reliable and one of the Colts' best offensive linemen. When quarterback Peyton Manning joined the team as a heralded rookie in 1998, it was Mandarich's job to protect the franchise player.

"I didn't play like a Pro Bowler, but I thought I played well and helped the Colts," Mandarich says. "I gave them everything I had. I dealt with a lot of issues in football, and for me, it made leaving the game a little easier. I didn't have that bad taste in my mouth when I retired for good."

These days, you can find Mandarich at Century Pines, the golf course he co-owns in Flamborough, Ontario, about 45 miles from Toronto. He bought the course in October 2000 with his Uncle Dinko and developer Iggy Kaneff.

Mandarich played golf casually as a teen but was bit by the bug late in his football career. He is an avid player with a career-best score of 81 and can hit his driver 325 yards, but he admits he doesn't always know where the ball is going. "I can get a hold of it," he says. "I can also hit it far out of bounds. I'll sacrifice 20 yards to keep it in the fairway, but my strength is length. My weakness is putting and chipping, because I don't practice as much as I should."

Mandarich is the general manager at Century Pines. He books outings, weddings, and parties, makes sure the golf shop is stocked with balls and tees, and oversees the restaurant and the maintenance of the eighteen-hole public course. It's not Augusta National, but it's his own little cathedral in the pines.

"This was a 5,000-yard, par-68 course. We shut down all of 2001, and we rebuilt the whole golf course," he says with obvious pride. "The old course was all bluegrass, and the greens were poa. We're bentgrass tee to green now. We put in cart paths and twenty-five new bunkers, all with Ohio white sand. We built a brand new clubhouse."

Some might consider booking weddings and taking tee-time reservations a demeaning job for a one-time college All-American football player. But Mandarich, the reformed wild child, appreciates everything he's got. "If it were to end today, I'd be okay," he says. "Do I want it to end? No. I'm enjoying life. There are still stresses in life, sure. But for the most part, you look at things in a relative fashion. You look at the hardships you went through in life and realize that the daily stresses now are nothing."

It seems an eternity ago that he blew into Green Bay, all bluster and ego, and left four years later a disillusioned and dispirited man.

"It seems," he says, "like a whole different lifetime for me."

He knows he's not highly regarded in Green Bay. The team has never invited him back for its annual Alumni Game, perhaps out of fear the fans would boo. But Mandarich doesn't hold a grudge and says he loved playing in Lambeau Field. "I

First and Foremost

The Packers' first-round picks in the National Football League draft since 1985:

1985—Ken Ruettgers, tackle, Southern California
1986—No pick
1987—Brent Fullwood, running back, Auburn
1988—Sterling Sharpe, wide receiver, South Carolina
1989—Tony Mandarich, tackle, Michigan State
1990—Tony Bennett, linebacker, Mississippi; Darrell Thompson, running back, Minnesota
1991—Vinnie Clark, cornerback, Ohio State
1992—Terrell Buckley, cornerback, Florida State
1993—Wayne Simmons, linebacker, Clemson; George Teague, safety, Alabama
1994—Aaron Taylor, guard, Notre Dame
1995—Craig Newsome, cornerback, Arizona State
1996—John Michels, tackle, Southern California
1997—Ross Verba, tackle, Iowa
1998—Vonnie Holliday, defensive tackle, North Carolina
1999—Antuan Edwards, cornerback, Clemson
2000—Bubba Franks, tight end, Miami
2001—Jamal Reynolds, defensive end, Florida State
2002—Javon Walker, wide receiver, Florida State
2003—Nick Barnett, linebacker, Oregon State
2004—Ahmad Carroll, cornerback, Arkansas

didn't want to go there at first because it was a small market and the Packers obviously weren't a very good team," he says. "But after I got there and got to experience the tradition and how loyal the fans were . . . to be able to call Lambeau Field my home field, that was an honor. It's an awesome place to play.

"I don't know if I'd go back if they asked me. Personally, I don't think they would invite me back. But if they invited me, yeah, I'd probably go back."

And if he could go back to 1989, would he do things differently?

"Absolutely," he says. "I would recommend to any rookie to play it low-key and just do the right things. In some ways I don't regret a lot of things because I learned a lot of lessons, not just about football but about life. In that sense I would say no, I don't regret anything because of where I am today."

Where he is today, is happy.

It's a very good place to be.

LeRoy Butler:
Safety First

It was a play LeRoy Butler had made hundreds and maybe thousands of times previously in his career. He came up from his safety position on a running play, squared up, and met the running back in the hole.

His technique was flawless, his timing perfect. In his thirteenth season with the Packers, the four-time Pro Bowl pick was nothing if not a sure tackler. But this tackle, on November 18, 2001, in a game against the Atlanta Falcons at Lambeau Field, would be his last in the National Football League.

Just before Butler collided with Atlanta's Maurice Smith, the running back lowered his head and drove the crown of his helmet into the top of Butler's left shoulder pad. The angle and force of the collision crushed a bone in Butler's shoulder socket and shattered his scapula.

Butler was helped off the field, wincing in pain, his left arm dangling awkwardly at his side. He would never play another game in the NFL. He tried to make a comeback in training camp before the 2002 season, but the bone in his shoulder hadn't healed properly and doctors told him he risked nerve damage if he took another similar hit.

He announced his retirement on July 18, 2002.

"It was a freak thing," Butler said. "Man, one play cost me another two years in the league. It was just the way that I hit the running back. I hit guys like that thousands of times. This particular day . . . the bone, it just shattered. It exploded.

"Had the top bone healed, the one in my shoulder, I could have played. It just didn't heal up. One more hit there, it could cut a nerve. It was too dangerous."

And so ended the career of one of the most talented, competitive, fearless, fun-loving, and fan-friendly players ever to don a Packers jersey. For more than a decade, Butler was the quarterback of the defense and in many ways the heart and soul of the team.

Sure, quarterback Brett Favre was the undisputed leader of the Pack in the 1990s, and for several seasons Reggie White was the larger-than-life minister of defense. But it was Butler's enthusiasm, loyalty, passion, and dedication—a rare combination in the modern professional athlete—that made him one of the most respected players in the locker room and around the league.

In for the Long Haul

LeRoy Butler played more games (181) than any defensive back in Packers history. When he retired after twelve seasons in 2002, only five players had worn the green and gold longer than Butler: Bart Starr (16 seasons), Ray Nitschke (15), Forrest Gregg (14), Charles "Buckets" Goldenberg (13), and Dave Hanner (13).

Butler's accomplishments form a portfolio worthy of Hall of Fame consideration. To list a few:

- He played in more games (181) than any other defensive back in Packers history and started all sixteen games in a season nine times.
- He was named to the 1990s NFL All-Decade team, as chosen by the Pro Football Hall of Fame.
- He finished his career with thirty-eight interceptions, fourth on the Packers' all-time list and just one behind third-place Herb Adderley, a Hall of Famer. When Butler retired, he was seventh among active players in interceptions.
- He played in four Pro Bowl games and started three in succession (1996–1998).
- He was one of only seven players to play with the same team from 1990 to 2001. (The others were Tim Brown and Steve Wisniewski with Oakland, Bruce Matthews with Tennessee, Darrell Green with Washington, Junior Seau with San Diego, and Emmitt Smith with Dallas.)

"My goal was to play my whole career with Green Bay," Butler said. "My goal was to look at all my football cards and see myself in a green jersey. That was a goal of mine, and for that to happen, I'm very proud."

Given the fact that Butler was born and raised in Jacksonville, Florida, and played college football at Florida State, his love for Green Bay and the Packers—the coldest of the cold-weather NFL franchises—is unusual in and of itself. Players with resumes and backgrounds comparable to Butler's usually take advantage of free agency to pursue their careers in warm-weather cities such as Miami or Tampa or in big media markets such as Los Angeles or New York.

Hindsight is 40-20

Butler fell two interceptions short of becoming the first player in National Football League history to record 40 interceptions and 20 sacks. He finished his career with 38 interceptions and 20½ sacks.

But Butler made his home in Green Bay, warmed quickly to the community and the fans, and never wanted to leave. More than once over the next dozen years, he would restructure his contract and defer millions in salary, both to ensure his future with the team and to help the franchise sign other players.

Not that he didn't have his doubts in the beginning.

"I knew nothing about Green Bay," he said. "I came from Florida State, where we averaged ten wins a season. Culturally, it was different. My first year we won [six] games and I was thinking, 'Man, this is terrible.' Plus, it was cold all the time.

"That first winter, I was driving a Nissan 300ZX, and the first snow we had, in November, I spun off the road. Some locals came in a truck and pulled me out. Any other city, you'd have to call roadside assistance, but in Green Bay everybody is like family and they help you out. They said, 'Look, LeRoy, we know who you are, second-round pick and all that. But you've got to buy a truck.' The next day, I got me a truck. I got rid of the 300ZX. I said, 'Either I'm going to look pretty and die, or I'm going to be safe.'

"The weather was a shock to my system. I didn't know how to put wood in the fireplace. Tim Harris [a linebacker with the team] showed me how to put the logs in there and light it. Next thing you know, I'm starting to be a Green Bay Packer. I'm wearing the winter coat, I've got the truck, the fireplace. I learned that in the winter, you stock up on food because if it snows, you can't get to the grocery store. I learned that you have to leave early to get to [team] meetings because your car may get stuck."

It was a huge adjustment for a kid from Florida who was used to warm weather and winning, but Butler's development as a player coincided with the Packers' return to prominence—and at times dominance—under Coach Mike Holmgren and General Manager Ron Wolf. After Green Bay went 4–12 in 1991, Butler's second year in the league and his first as a starter, he never again experienced a losing season.

But let's start at the beginning, because the fact that Butler even made it to the NFL is something of a miracle in itself.

Born with severely misaligned feet, he spent much of his childhood in casts or braces and at times in a wheelchair. His feet were so pigeon-toed, doctors had to break bones in them and realign them on three occasions.

"It started when I was three years old," Butler said. "Between the ages of three and eight, the doctors broke my feet three times. They put them in casts and as soon as they took off the casts, my feet turned right back in. Then they'd have to reposition them. It was very painful. So many hours a day, I had to sit in a wheelchair because if I stood up, it hurt."

One day, Butler's older sister was late for a date, came running down the stairs, and tripped over Butler's wheelchair. It tipped over and the casts on his feet broke. In a real-life version of the scene from the movie *Forrest Gump*, Butler stood up and started to walk. There was no pain in his feet.

"I just got up and everybody was kind of screaming," he said, smiling at the memory. "My mom said, 'Stand up. You can walk!' And I started running. It was just like out of *Forrest Gump*, except nobody threw any rocks at me."

Butler broke the chains of his medical condition and his impoverished childhood in the Blodgett Homes project in Jacksonville and became an exceptional football player at Robert E. Lee High School, where he was a prep All-American. In his senior year he made 139 tackles, intercepted 5 passes and averaged 15.3 yards per rushing attempt in 31 carries as a running back.

At Florida State he was a three-year starter at right cornerback, totaling 194 tackles, 9 interceptions, 2 fumble recoveries, 3 forced fumbles, 1 sack, and 14 passes broken up for the Seminoles.

In 1988 Butler stunned 82,500 Clemson fans by rushing 78 yards on a fake punt from the Seminoles 21 yard line. The play set up a game-winning field goal with less than two minutes left for a 24–21 Florida State victory.

The Packers had plenty of needs going into the 1990 NFL college draft. After taking linebacker Tony Bennett of Mississippi and running back Darrell Thompson of Minnesota with their two first-round picks, they tabbed Butler in the second round. He was the forty-eighth player drafted overall.

"I was hoping to go to Dallas, because that was my favorite team, or maybe Pittsburgh," Butler said. "But [head coach] Lindy Infante, who I owe a lot to, gave me the opportunity. Lindy and [general manager] Tom Braatz and [secondary coach] Dick Jauron were the only ones that wanted to draft me. Everybody else said, 'We need a linebacker. We need a wide receiver.' Lindy said, 'Look, if this guy is available, we've got to take him. This guy can play twelve years for us.'

"Lindy would sometimes let the other guys make the draft picks and stay out of it. But when they had a chance to draft me, he came in there and voiced his opinion."

Butler played in all sixteen regular-season games as a rookie in 1990 and shared the team lead in interceptions with three. The next season, he started all sixteen games at right cornerback. He had three interceptions, and each one ended an opponent's drive deep in Packers territory. Already, he was showing big-play capabilities.

In 1992, Holmgren's first year as head coach, Butler moved to strong safety and flourished under new defensive coordinator Ray Rhodes. "Ray was kind of like a father figure to me," Butler said. "He taught me to have a nasty attitude on the field. I appreciated that, because I was always known as a nice guy. I smiled a lot. But on the field, I changed. Ray used to call me the 'Hulk.' Then I started making plays. So I owe a lot to him."

Butler had 111 tackles and 6 interceptions in 1993. On December 26, in a game against the Los Angeles Raiders at Lambeau Field, Butler did something that will forever live in Packers lore. That was the day he invented the "Lambeau Leap."

Let's let Butler set the scene:

"Man, the windchill factor was like twenty-eight below zero," Butler said. "I remember seeing [Raiders receiver] Tim Brown get off the bus on the news the night before the game. He was like, 'Man, it's cold here.' Then when the game started, it looked like they didn't even want to play.

"Vince Evans was the quarterback. He threw the ball to the running back in the flat. I hit him and caused a fumble. Reggie White picked it up and started running with it, and some guy, I think it was Steve Wisniewski, started to pull him down. Reggie and I made eye contact. [Packers linebacker] Bryce

LeRoy Butler was the consummate professional and one of the best safeties in the National Football League in the 1990s. Intelligent and versatile, he was equally adept at covering receivers, tackling running backs, and sacking the quarterback. (Courtesy Sports Marketing & Management Group)

Paup was laying on the ground in front of me, so I jumped over him and Reggie pitched me the ball as he was falling.

"I'm running down the sideline and it's hunting season, so I see all this orange [hunting vests] in the stands behind the end zone. I just started pointing, like, 'I'm going to jump.' When I jumped up there, the fans grabbed me, and, man, it was so loud. It was just something spontaneous. The crowd, even through the extra point and the kickoff, they were still standing, going nuts. It was awesome. Thinking about it now gives me goose bumps."

Butler's leap started a trend at Lambeau. Any Packer who scored a touchdown invariably sprinted through the end zone and launched himself into the crowd, where he was swallowed by back-slapping, beer-slurping fans.

The Packers were so good on their home field that the leap became a regular occurrence, which surely eroded the confidence of opposing teams. Ten years later, many Packers still celebrated touchdowns by doing the "Lambeau Leap."

In 1994 Fritz Shurmur replaced Rhodes as defensive coordinator and began to design defensive schemes to take advantage of Butler's unique skills. Shurmur brought the safety up to the line of scrimmage, where he helped in run support, dropped back into coverage, or rushed the quarterback. Opponents had to account for number 36, but they never knew where he would be or what he would do.

"If it wasn't for Fritz, I don't know if I would be on the [NFL] All-Decade team, played in Pro Bowls, or made All-Pro, because he put me in position to make those plays," Butler said. "Ray Rhodes switched me to safety. Fritz Shurmur continued to develop me.

"No safety was blitzing until Fritz came around with that plan. That's why I got more sacks than any defensive back that played the game. Before that, nobody was doing it. Everybody wanted to have two safeties back, but we proved that you can play up and play back at the same time."

In 1995 Butler had a career-high 117 tackles, a career-high 6½ half sacks, and 5 interceptions, one of which he returned 90 yards for a touchdown. The more big plays Butler made, the more pressure Holmgren put on him to make big plays. "I think it had a lot to do with Coach Holmgren, because of the pressure he put on me," Butler said. "He put pressure on me not to be some regular stiff safety, some guy who just stood in the middle. He put pressure on me to be something special. He said I always had to make the right play, that the team depended on me. He had me thinking if I didn't make those plays, we would lose.

"Oh, I loved it. I really loved it. I thrived on that pressure."

As Butler became a leader on the field, he also grew into his role as a leader off the field. He became one of the best quotes in the locker room, a player whom the media knew would speak with insight and candor, win or lose. Sometimes, his truthfulness got him in trouble with Holmgren. But Butler took his role as a team spokesman seriously.

"Some of the stuff I said, [Holmgren] didn't want the media to know," he said. "I just felt like that was the only way I could talk to the fans. When we got beat by Indianapolis [in 1997], they were like 0–10, and we were dominating people at the time. Holmgren warned us about a letdown. After the game, everyone just left. I remember the media coming in the locker room, and I wanted to have the opportunity to say that we stunk the place up. Because when people pick up the paper on the way to work the next morning, and they're drinking their coffee, they want to know how stupid we played and how dumb it was. When you explain that, when you're hard on yourself, you'd be amazed at how easy people can be on you.

"And other guys appreciate you dealing with the media, because they don't want to do it. They just want to do it when we win the big games. Then they've got their chest out. But I thought people respect you when you're always there. I used to look forward to Wednesdays and Fridays, being with the media and having some humor with it. The other team would read my quotes. And Holmgren would say, 'Why did you say that?' I'd say, 'Hey, that's just me.' "

The Packers became a very good team in the mid-1990s, but they couldn't get past the Dallas Cowboys in the playoffs. Finally, in 1996 they put it all together, compiling a 13–3 regular-season record, then crushing San Francisco and Carolina in the playoffs to reach Super Bowl XXXI in New Orleans, where they beat the New England Patriots, 35–21, to win their first NFL title since 1967.

"I remember being very jealous of Deion Sanders when he was in Dallas and San Francisco, winning those Super Bowls," Butler said. "I thought, 'Man, I'm never going to win a Super Bowl.' When we actually did, I was on top of the world. It was just awesome. Because when I first got to Green Bay, I thought there was no way possible I would ever get there."

The Packers returned to Super Bowl XXXII the next season but lost to the Denver Broncos, 31–24.

Butler continued to be a productive player, but he started slowing down a bit in the late 1990s. More and more, the Packers shifted some of his duties to free safety Darren Sharper, a younger, more athletic player. Sharper was gifted physically but made his share of mental mistakes. Butler was content to play deep and prevent the long pass, while turning Sharper loose to roam the field and make plays on the ball.

"Basically, I was just the quarterback of the defense," Butler said. "I didn't need to make all the superman plays I used to make. I was okay with that. I never considered myself a speedster, but you lose a step as you get older. It was more important for me to be in the right place at the right time towards the end of my career. Darren was a better athlete at that point, and if I could put him in those positions, we'd have a better chance to win the game.

"My role was to make sure everybody was lined up and to get to the middle of the field and make sure there was nothing deep. Let Sharper do all the blitzing and intercepting and fun stuff. I didn't have a problem with that."

In 2001 the Packers were 6–2 under second-year Coach Mike Sherman when Butler went down with his career-ending shoulder injury. He spent the rest of the season on the sideline and retired the next summer.

Butler did some work for ESPN and took the time to write an autobiography, aptly titled, *The LeRoy Butler Story: From Wheelchair to Lambeau Leap*. But he missed the camaraderie of the locker room and the thrill of big games . . . and still does.

"I really miss those Monday night games," he said. "The games that the Packers lost, I felt kind of helpless. Even the last game [a loss to the Atlanta Falcons in the 2002 playoffs], I just felt like had I been there, it would have been different. I worked at ESPN, so I stayed close to the game. But there's nothing like those Monday night games and those twelve o'clock, high noon games. Those are the ones I miss the most."

Butler also took a job in coaching after he retired, but not with the Packers. He served as the assistant head coach at Ribault High School in Jacksonville, Florida. He interviewed for a front-office job with the Jacksonville Jaguars but longed to work for the Packers organization in some capacity. "The only thing I'm disappointed in is that I put in twelve years, and now I've just sort of disappeared from the organization," Butler said. "I kind of wish I would have some kind of tie with them. The fans ask me, 'Why aren't you coaching? Why aren't you in the front office?' I tell them, 'Wait a minute, I can't just go up there and do it. They have to ask me.'"

In 2004 the Packers asked. Butler agreed to assist Sherman and the entire organization in a role called "special assignments." Butler hopes it will serve as his entry into a full-time coaching job.

But it is his greatest hope that someday his number 36 jersey will be retired and his name will be put up in yellow lettering on the rim of Lambeau Field. Only the team's Hall of Fame members are so honored. "That would mean everything to me," Butler said. "But if they ever do give out number 36 again, I hope the guy who wears it knows I was one of the leaders of the team."

It would not exactly be a secret.

The One and Only

When quarterback Brett Favre failed to show up for his postgame news conference after the Packers were eliminated by the Atlanta Falcons in the first round of the National Football League playoffs on January 4, 2002, fans from Wausau to Wauwatosa held their collective breath. In the decade that Favre had been entrenched as the starting quarterback, he had failed to appear at his regular postgame press conference on only a few rare occasions. Win or lose, Favre almost always could be counted on for candid and insightful observations about the team's performance that day.

What did this no-show mean?

Packers fans feared the worst.

During the 2002 season Favre's name and retirement had been mentioned in the same sentence—on several occasions by Favre himself—for the first time in his career. Yes, the quarterback said in interviews, he thought about what it would be like to hang up his cleats and retire to the good life. He thought about what it would be like to play golf year-round, to hunt and fish whenever he felt like it, to while away the hours on his tractor at home in Hattiesburg, Mississippi.

Favre admitted that his mind occasionally wandered in meetings or film sessions, something that never happened earlier in his career. He had no problem getting fired up on game day, but the tedium of practices challenged his focus. As the undisputed team leader, Favre knew that his practice habits set the tone for the Packers, and while no one had noticed any less energy or enthusiasm from him, it was becoming more difficult for him to bounce around at practice like a sugar-buzzed twelve-year-old.

Plus, the accumulated aches, pains, strains, and sprains were taking longer to heal in the off-season. He wondered how much more his body could take, and whether a career-threatening injury—the one he had managed to avoid for twelve seasons—was lurking around the corner. Favre wanted to go out on his own terms, and a knee strain he had suffered earlier in the 2002 season, when Washington Redskins linebacker LaVar Arrington sacked him and his leg twisted awkwardly beneath him, was a wake-up call. Favre was carted off the field that day, holding a towel over his face to hide his tears.

Miraculously, the knee strain was minor. Fortuitously, Green Bay had a bye the next week. And incredibly, just fifteen days after it appeared that his season might be over, Favre wore a brace on his knee and played in a *Monday Night Football* game . . . and led Green Bay to a resounding victory over the Miami Dolphins.

But his brush with serious injury had fueled speculation that retirement no longer was just an abstract idea for the most durable player at his position in NFL history. Favre added to the speculation by being vague about his plans, and the fact that he had put his house in Green Bay up for sale did nothing to comfort Packers fans.

Then, alarmingly, Favre blew off his news conference after the shocking and bitterly disappointing loss to the Falcons at Lambeau Field, where the Packers had never lost a playoff game. A team spokesman said the quarterback would address the media two days later.

Could this be it? Could Favre be getting ready to announce he was leaving the game . . . and leaving the Packers in the lurch?

Favre was forty-five minutes late for the scheduled news conference, which was aired live on Milwaukee television stations. Every five or ten minutes, the stations would break away from regularly scheduled programming to show a live shot of an empty podium. If you were not familiar with the Packers' incredible popularity in Wisconsin or Favre's status as the state's most revered athlete, this would have struck you as comical.

Finally, Favre strolled into the media auditorium in the bowels of Lambeau Field, wearing his trademark baseball cap and a multiday growth of stubble. While he chose not to answer "yes" when asked directly if he would play another season, he gave every indication that he would return in 2003. "We have nothing but great things to look forward to here," he said. "I don't know how many years it will be, but it's one of those decisions that's really made easier when you think about it, coming back.

"I don't have anything to prove. I know that. Nothing at all. And that makes it easier for me. I can just play. I realize the things that I have to be thankful for. Health is one of them. And the way I played the last few years is encouraging. . . . It just makes my decision so much easier to come back."

His words meant two things: The franchise and its far-flung fans could count on Favre for at least one more year, but—and this was the sobering half of the equation—the team needed to take a hard look at replacing him in the not-too-distant future.

Mike Sherman, who wore the dual hats of coach and general manager, said in his own postseason news conference that he would consider taking a quarterback in the early rounds of the 2003 NFL draft. He brought in Ron Wolf, former general manager, to help evaluate the talent. The coaches then could groom the young quarterback to take Favre's place when the inevitable occurred.

Favre would go into his thirteenth season with his place secure among the greatest quarterbacks in NFL history.

Let's start with the numbers, which add up to a first-ballot ticket into the Pro Football Hall of Fame in Canton, Ohio. Going into the 2003 season, Favre had completed 3,652 of 5,993 passes for 42,285 yards, with 314 touchdowns and 188 interceptions. He had rushed 451 times for 1,632 yards and 12 touchdowns.

In 17 playoff games he had completed 338 of 594 passes, with 30 touchdowns and 21 interceptions.

But all those numbers added together pale in comparison with this one: 173. That's the number of regular-season games Favre had started consecutively, easily a record for NFL quarterbacks and among the all-time tough-guy streaks in any sport. Throw in the playoff games, and the streak was at 190.

Considering Favre had been sacked 376 times in his career, including playoff games, and probably had been hit or knocked to the ground after releasing the ball at least 1,500 more times, it was truly an impressive streak.

"Why hasn't Brett Favre been knocked out of the lineup with a concussion, you know?" asked former Cincinnati Bengals quarterback Boomer Esiason, now a television analyst. "How come he hasn't missed a game with a sprained ankle or been knocked out with a rib injury? Because he won't let it happen. It's partly body makeup, but I think it's mental makeup, too. He says, 'Nobody is going to hurt me.' "

Favre first earned his tough-guy reputation at Southern Mississippi, where he led the Golden Eagles to twenty-nine victories and two bowl triumphs in four years. Just weeks before the start of his senior season, he suffered serious internal injuries in a car accident. On August 7, 1990, doctors had to remove thirty inches of his intestines, but he shocked his coaches and teammates by returning to the starting lineup one month later (September 8) and leading Southern Mississippi to an upset over Alabama.

The Atlanta Falcons picked Favre in the second round of the 1991 NFL draft. He was the thirty-third pick overall and the third quarterback taken, after Dan McGwire and Todd Marinovich.

Favre's rookie season was largely a wasted year, unless you count his off-the-field exploits. He was active for just three games and played in two, attempting five passes without a completion and throwing two interceptions. But if Favre couldn't be the Falcons' starting quarterback, he at least could be the life of the party. For a fun-loving, twenty-two-year-old kid from the tiny backwater burg of Kiln, Mississippi, a little money and a lot of time could be a potent combination.

Favre Throws to . . . Favre!

Here's a great trivia question: Which player was on the receiving end of Brett Favre's first National Football League pass completion?

The answer: Brett Favre.

On September 13, 1992, in a game against the Tampa Bay Buccaneers, Favre's first pass attempt with the Packers was deflected. He caught the ball and was tackled for a loss of 7 yards.

By his own admission years later, Favre "probably drank up Atlanta" that year. He certainly didn't burn up the NFL. He was so immature and irresponsible that he failed to show up for the Falcons' team photograph. The coach at the time, Jerry Glanville, quickly ran out of patience with his wild-child quarterback. Despite Favre's one-in-a-million arm, there was no indication that he was destined for greatness.

Everything changed—for Favre, for the Falcons, for the Green Bay Packers, and for the NFL—when Wolf traded a first-round draft pick to Atlanta for the unproven quarterback on February 10, 1992.

Favre admitted he couldn't have found Green Bay on a map. Packers fans wondered how this raw-boned, undisciplined player could be worth a first-round pick. But with Wolf's sharp eye for talent, and first-year Coach Mike Holmgren's knack for tutoring quarterbacks—he had worked with Joe Montana and Steve Young in San Francisco—Favre's worth soon became evident.

Favre got serious about his career and buckled down under Holmgren's stern leadership. His talents proved to be perfect for the West Coast offense. At 6'2" and 225 pounds, he had ideal size for a pocket passer, but his mobility, uncanny sense for avoiding pressure, and rare ability to improvise when a play broke down made him unique.

Favre could throw with pinpoint accuracy on the run, either right or left. His arm strength was incredible: With a flick of his wrist, he could easily deliver the ball 50 yards downfield while backpedaling, and he took a perverse delight in breaking or dislocating receivers' fingers with his bullets. Nimble, if not speedy, he could scramble for a first down if all else failed. The ultimate team player, he would sprint down the field after throwing a touchdown pass and jump into the

Quarterback Brett Favre after a victory at Lambeau Field. Favre took over for an injured Don Majkowski in 1992 and didn't miss a game through the 2003 season. (Vernon J. Biever Photo)

arms of the receiver, or sometimes even tackle him, a practice that Holmgren frowned on and eventually outlawed.

Then there was Favre's toughness. He basically was wired to be a middle linebacker but wound up with a quarterback's body. He bounced up from vicious hits and patted defenders on the butt for trying to take off his head. He talked trash. He relished blocking defensive ends on reverses.

And he was totally, completely unpredictable, which drove defensive coordinators crazy. They couldn't prepare for everything Favre could do, and that was his edge.

In the Packers' third game of the 1992 season, against the Cincinnati Bengals at Lambeau Field, Favre was summoned from the bench to replace starter Don Majkowski, who had suffered an ankle injury. He led Green Bay to an electrifying, come-from-behind 24–23 victory, throwing the game-winning 35-yard touchdown pass to obscure receiver Kitrick Taylor with thirteen seconds left.

The rest, as they say, is history.

Over the next decade Favre would win the league's most valuable player award an unprecedented three times. He would lead the Packers to two Super Bowl appearances, including a triumph over the New England Patriots in Super Bowl XXXI in New Orleans in 1997. He would become one of the most recognizable and most popular figures in sports, even appearing in a cameo role in the hit movie *There's Something About Mary*. He would become, in the words of former Bengal Esiason, "a National Football League treasure."

"And he plays for America's Team," Esiason added. "I don't care what people say about the Dallas Cowboys, the Green Bay Packers are America's Team."

Not that it has always been easy to be Brett Favre or to play like him.

Along the way the quarterback has battled an addiction to the powerful painkiller Vicodin; watched in sorrow as one of his best friends, former Packers tight end Mark Chmura, was charged with and eventually acquitted of sexual assault; soldiered on through an assortment of injuries to his back, arm, feet, ankles, and just about every other part of his anatomy; played for three head coaches (Mike Holmgren, Ray Rhodes, and Mike Sherman); and endured rocky times in his marriage to Deanna.

He has emerged from it all wiser and more mature, at once more confident and more at peace with himself. He is one of a handful of superstars around which the NFL builds its image. It is no coincidence that his number 4 Packers jersey annually ranks among the top two or three in the league in sales of replica jerseys. Favre has made the transition from wide-eyed gunslinger to consummate professional, and he is enormously respected by his teammates and almost universally admired by opposing players.

"He's been in so many situations in games that he knows what to do in any situation," said former Miami Dolphins quarterback Dan Marino, who holds many of the passing records Favre is chasing. "That comes with time and playing. In the early '90s when he was playing well, it was just arm strength. Now he's been in every possible situation a quarterback can see. He's seen every defensive alignment, every blitz. He's won coming from behind, with big leads, in bad weather. He's lost some tough ones.

"The other thing is the heart that guy has. That influences the rest of the team and their attitude."

Joe Theismann, the former Washington Redskins quarterback and now an analyst for ESPN, said Favre's ability to inspire confidence in his teammates was perhaps his most important quality.

"He has the belief of the players he plays with," Theismann said. "They believe that as long as Brett is under center, they have the ability to win every game."

Esiason and former Dallas Cowboys quarterback Troy Aikman both see a maturity in Favre, on and off the field, that has helped him overcome the accumulated aches and pains and emotional ups and downs of a long career.

"He's certainly not the carefree player he was in '92, when he took over for Don Majkowski and beat us," said Esiason, the former Bengal. "He's maybe not as reckless personally as he once was."

Said Aikman: "I think he's been making better decisions the last couple of years. There was a time early in his career when he would come out and start firing the ball around the yard and get himself in trouble. I think he's not as willing to try to hit the home run on every single play now. There's a maturity in his game, and I think his maturity off the field is just as important."

Only two quarterbacks in NFL history (Marino and Fran Tarkenton) have thrown more touchdown passes than Favre. Only four have completed more passes, and only five have thrown for more yards. Favre ranks fifth in regular-season victories since the NFL–AFL merger, behind John Elway, Marino, Tarkenton, and Joe Montana.

Inarguably, Favre ranks among the top ten quarterbacks in NFL history. But how high on that list does he belong? It's a subjective question, to be sure, but those who have played quarterback and achieved considerable success in the NFL are in a unique position to answer it.

"My top three would be Joe Montana, Brett Favre, and Steve Young," said Theismann, a Super Bowl–winning quarterback with the Washington Redskins. "I think the demands

Cold and Calculating

When the Atlanta Falcons upset the Packers in the 2002 NFL playoffs, a remarkable streak by quarterback Brett Favre came to an end. Favre, a native of Kiln, Mississippi, had compiled a 35–0 record at Lambeau Field (6–0 in playoff games) when the temperature at game time was thirty-four degrees or colder.

of today's game are different than they used to be. When I played, the Bob Grieses, Sonny Jurgensons, Dan Foutses . . . they were all great, but I would never list them among the greatest ever. And not to take anything away from a Johnny Unitas or a Bart Starr, but to me, the guys who have been MVPs, who have won championships, and won in a lot of different situations and circumstances are the guys I put at the top of the list."

Esiason ranks Favre even higher.

"I would take Brett number one," he said. "I would probably take Joe Montana number two. Then I don't know. The third one would probably be Terry Bradshaw. The guy won four Super Bowls. When I think back on Bradshaw and the Pittsburgh Steelers, I remember you had this feeling that something big was going to happen on every play. It's the same feeling I have watching Brett. You know, shallow crossing route, wait a second, he's got a guy going down the sideline . . . boom, touchdown.

"If you put it in the context of who is the one quarterback you would want behind center for one season during his prime . . . I would be hard-pressed not to want Brett. Does the guy make people around him better and do his teammates have the ultimate respect and admiration for him? When you're talking about Brett, the answer is absolutely yes."

No one knows how much longer Favre will play, probably including Favre himself. If he can stay on top of his game physically and retain his passion for his job, he'll keep playing. If injuries or waning desire become factors, he'll retire. Those who know him claim it wouldn't matter if he was one touchdown or 1 yard short of breaking Marino's records. When Favre can no longer play at a championship level, there will be no convincing him to stay another day.

Aikman said the Packers' success under Mike Sherman could help keep Favre focused and interested. "The hardest thing for me was not physical limitations, it was where we were as a football team," Aikman said, referring to the decline of the Dallas Cowboys toward the end of his career. "After you've reached some level of success, and then you wade around in mediocrity, that's hard to deal with. Truth be told, I couldn't deal with it any longer. That's what drove me out.

"Brett is fortunate. Mike Sherman has done a great job. The team is getting better. If the team was not playing well, it would be harder for him to maintain his enthusiasm."

About the Author

Gary D'Amato has been a sports reporter at the *Milwaukee Journal Sentinel* since 1990, covering a variety of sports, including Packers football and two Super Bowl games. He is the author of two other books on the Packers: *The Packer Tapes* with Domenic Gentile, and *Mudbaths and Bloodbaths: The Inside Story of the Bears–Packers Rivalry* with Cliff Christl (Prairie Oak Press).